I0022225

Relational Listening: A Handbook

Cross-Culturally Resonant Gateways into Human Relational Experience

Lawrence E. Hedges
PhD, PsyD, ABPP

Listening Perspectives Press
ORANGE, California
2018 / 2023

Copyright © 2018 Lawrence E. Hedges
© 2018 International Psychotherapy Institute (digital)
© 2023 Listening Perspectives Press
ISBN 9780999454725

All Rights Reserved

This book contains material protected under International and Federal Copyright Laws and Treaties. This book is intended for personal use only. Any unauthorized reprint or use of this material is prohibited. No part of this book may be used in any commercial manner without express permission of the author. Scholarly use of quotations must have proper attribution to the published work. This work may not be deconstructed, reverse engineered or reproduced in any other format.

Created in the United States of America

For my colleagues in
Shanghai, Bejing, Hangzhoa, Chenqdu, Nanjing,
Qingdao, Shenzhen, Lanzhou,
Hong Kong, Shenyang, and Macau
at the Chinese American Psychoanalytic Alliance

陈天星 Chen Tian Xing (Simon)　　　胡蘋 Hu Ping (Coral)

贾晋超 Jia Jin Chao (Jack)　　　江岚 Jiang Lan (Sand)

刘琳娜 Liu Lin Na (Linna)　　　罗鑫垚 Luo Xin Yao (Nancy)

宋静 Song Jing (Jocye)　　　唐芹 Tang Qin (Mary)

SONG Xinxin (Athena)　　　YU Guoyu (Jade)

ZHONG Ou　　　KANG Jianxi (Kevin)

CHEN Shanshan (Amanda)　　　WU Bing (Winnie)

QU Lili (Lily)　　　LI Ying (Anna)

XING Xiaochun (Jane)　　　ZHOU Yanyu (Fish)

NG Kwun Shing　　　Kwun Shingdum (Ernest)

LONG Xiaofeng (Azalea)　　　NIE Xiaojing (Ginger)

ZHAO Jie (Claire)　　　LIU Xiaomeng (Judy)

PENG Jun (Chloe)　　　SHAO Zhouying (Zoe)

LIU Fangsong (Peter)　　　LUAN Xue Bin (Gene)

CHU Yun Pik (Marion)

Acknowledgments

This handbook has evolved in collaboration with the following professional colleagues:

Audrey Seaton-Bacon	Laura Haynes
Brendan Baer	Mauri-Lynne Heller
Linda Barnhurst	Ken Kaisch
Judith Besteman	Marlene Laping
Lori Burri	Laurie Lucas
Nancy Caltagirone	Christine McMahon
John D. Carter	Lisa Maurel
Joseph Chun	Robert Glenn Mowbray
Doug Citro	Yana Newberg
Janis Corbin	Priscilla Newton
Cheryl Graybill-Dale	James Tobin
Jolyn Davidson	Ted Trubenbach
Robert Davison	Carla Rather
Antoinette M. Eimers	Jeff Schwieger
Margarite Fairweather	Charles Spicer
Terence Ford	Daniel Uribe
Ann Goldman	Sheree Riley-Violon
Roxy Green	Vera Viss
Susan Harris	Robert Whitcomb

Special thanks goes to
Ray Calabrese, Daniel Uribe,
Monica Mello, Greggory Moore, and Jason Aronson
for their ongoing support of my work.
And as always, Melonie Bell's editorial work is superb!

TABLE OF CONTENTS

Foreword

Dr. Larry Hedges has spent a professional lifetime cultivating the art of listening to his clients and teaching other psychoanalytically oriented clinicians to do the same.

To that end, more than 40 years ago Larry introduced to the mental health community his wildly popular *Listening Perspectives in Psychotherapy*—a groundbreaking gem of a book in which he, already extremely well-versed in the various schools of psychoanalytic thought, made use of *developmental metaphors* to bring to life the four distinct types of increasingly complex patterns of self and other relatedness (the organizing experience, the symbiotic experience, the selfother experience, and the independence experience) that he had identified as pivotal in psychoanalytic work. Part of Larry's genius lay in his courageous recognition that these patterns of relational expectation would inform not only the client's transference and resistance but also the therapist's countertransference and counter-resistance.

Shortly thereafter, Larry created his Listening Perspectives Study Center—a continuing education program devoted to providing mental health professionals with the opportunity to deepen and broaden their theoretical and clinical understanding of how to work analytically with the mutual enactments that will inevitably emerge between client and therapist as their relationship evolves and their relational patterns come into play.

Twenty books later, in this brilliantly accessible *Relational Perspectives Handbook* Larry is now offering the reader a crisply streamlined overview of his four Relational Listening Perspectives, with a few modifications and subtle refinements. He makes a fascinating distinction that I had never quite put together. He starts by noting that many psychotherapies in vogue today (e.g., positive psychology, supportive therapy, acceptance and commitment therapy, mindfulness meditation, and cognitive behavior therapy) focus on *building up* adaptive capacity by fostering neuroplasticity and the creation of new synaptic linkages in the brain, which of course is all well and good.

But Larry goes on to compare these psychotherapies to psychoanalytic therapy, which focuses first on *breaking down* the client's limiting relational patterns—patterns that had been interfering with healthy relatedness—and then on *working through* these constricting patterns in the context of the therapy relationship. This continuously evolving *analytic process* involves negotiating the various transference/ countertransference entanglements that will continuously emerge at the *intimate edge*[1] between client and therapist—such that there can be eventual transformation of underlying relational fears, revision of templates and scripts, and expansion of relational possibilities.

In other words, whereas many psychotherapies focus on *building up*, psychoanalytic therapy focuses on *breaking down* (destabilization / disruption) so that, by way of *working through* the co-created relational dynamics between client and therapist, there can be a *building up* (restabilization/ repair)—but this time at a higher level of nuanced understanding, relational capacity, and developmental complexity.

---

[1] Ehrenberg, D. B. (1992). *The Intimate Edge: Extending the Reach of Psychoanalytic Interaction*. New York: W.W. Norton & Company.

In truth, the way that Larry—a psychoanalyst par excellence—teaches, and does, psychoanalytic therapy makes me proud to call myself a psychoanalyst. Unlike some writers, he truly practices what he preaches and he articulates the analytic process so beautifully and compellingly.

One of the things about Larry that is most intriguing is that he has always managed somehow to stay ahead of the curve. He is a real trailblazer—but ever humble, heartfelt, authentic, soulful, compassionate, and human. Although 3,000 miles separate us (his home is in the Los Angeles area whereas mine is in Boston), I have had the privilege and pleasure of calling Larry both my dear friend and my esteemed colleague for many decades now, and we have found creative ways to stay in touch over the years.

Most importantly, I owe Larry a huge debt of gratitude for his gentle and kind but firm insistence that I expand my formulation of the three *Modes of Therapeutic Action*—that, for decades, had formed the centerpiece for my own conceptual framework—to include an additional *Mode*! I resisted as best I could. Here was my brilliant colleague, who pretty much knew everything there was to know about everything psychoanalytic, asking me to revamp my entire methodology, one about which I had been writing many books and teaching for more than thirty years!

But, a few years ago, I finally relented and came to accept the fact that, in order to round out the infrastructure of the system that I had so painstakingly constructed over the course of the previous decades, I really did need to supplement the *structural conflict* of my Model 1, the *structural deficit* of my Model 2, and the *relational conflict* of my Model 3 with a Model 4, the focus of which would be *relational deficit.*

I will indeed be eternally grateful to my dear friend Larry for having made it his business to know my work so well that he knew what was missing. Perhaps it was there all along, just waiting to be found; but I am quite sure that I would never have found it but for Larry's generous and loving insistence that I keep looking.

Let me hasten to say that, adding the existential-humanistic perspective of Model 4 to my conceptual framework for the therapeutic action has resulted in a profound deepening and broadening of both my theoretical framework and my clinical work! My students and my clients are its benefactors. I thank you, Larry, from the bottom of my heart for the incredible gift that you have given me.

It is therefore a privilege and a pleasure for me to be now in the position of being able to write this Foreword for your masterfully crafted *Relational Perspectives Handbook*—a concise and deeply satisfying summary of your massive body of work, which has spanned more than four decades. Your landmark contributions to the psychoanalytic literature have clearly withstood the test of time and will most certainly remain at the forefront going forward.

Martha Stark, MD
Faculty, Harvard Medical School
Author, 7 Books on Psychoanalytic Theory and Practice

Author's Introduction

This is the 20th book in a series authored and edited by myself establishing and expanding Relational Listening Perspectives.

This *Handbook* surveys a massive clinical research project extending over 45 years and participated in by more than 400 psychotherapists in case conferences, reading groups and seminars at the Listening Perspectives Study Center and the Newport Psychoanalytic Institute in the Southern California area.

My lectures from the 1970s were integrated into the first book in the series, *Listening Perspective in Psychotherapy* published by Jason Aronson in 1983. When I sent my first manuscript to Dr. Aronson, he immediately grasped the important epistemological shift in psychotherapy thinking that the book represented and sent a contract back by return mail. Later, in 2002 I was lecturing at the Washington Square Psychoanalytic Institute in New York City with Jason and his wife Joyce in attendance. Afterwards at dinner at the Four Seasons Jason remarked, "Larry, these days everybody is talking relational—relational, relational, relational! You were doing that more than 20 years ago and no one seemed to catch on!"

Listening Perspectives was widely praised for its comprehensive survey of 100 years of psychoanalytic studies and a 20th-anniversary edition came out in 2003. But the important aspect of the book—that the studies were organized according to four different human relatedness listening perspectives of different developmental complexity—went largely unnoticed. Also generally unattended was the critical epistemological shift to perspectivalism which since that time has become better understood. The subsequent books participated in by numerous therapists expand and elaborate these perspectives for working clinicians.[2]

This *Handbook* is necessarily largely "telegraphic" in the sense that there is no way for a short communication to convey the clinical richness and the depth of personal participation engaged in by the many therapists and clients who have contributed their remarkable talents and painstaking work over the years. This book is also "telegraphic" in the sense that the ideas of hundreds of creative clinicians, theoreticians, and writers have been quoted and cited throughout the series and only a few can be mentioned in such a brief overview. For this I must apologize in advance to all of the many people whose thoughts and ideas are integrated into this summarizing text and who are not here credited in conventional ways. However, throughout this *Handbook* I point to the various contributions in our series that deal in detail with various topics and it is in those books that proper credits and references appear. Likewise, it has not been possible to include clinical material from psychotherapy adventures in this *Handbook* but the other books in the series are rich with clinical contributions from many different psychotherapists with different orientations and ways of working.

Finally, although the perspectives and the clinical work supporting them have been derived from a century of mostly psychoanalytic studies, the work of this research project has been to adapt and expand those in-depth findings to help clinicians of all theoretical and clinical persuasions with their work—especially with difficult-to-treat clients.

---

[2] Nineteen of these books are listed in the references.

Dr. Aronson has for some time been urging me to write a handbook overview of the entire project. But it has been my experience of leading video case conference groups in China that has inspired me not only to summarize but to demonstrate that the Relational Listening Perspectives approach is essentially cross-culturally resonant.

I hope this overview inspires you to seek out some of the other contributions of our project mostly published by Jason Aronson and Routledge, although many are now offered as free downloads on the International Psychotherapy Institute's website, freepsychotherapybooks.org.

Thanks for your interest and patience in checking us out!

Lawrence Hedges
Orange, California

Part One

WHY CONSTRUCT LISTENING PERSPECTIVES?

The Infinite Complexity of Human Mind

We now realize that the most complex phenomenon in the known universe is the human mind. Understanding this infinite complexity of mind, we now see the impossibility of the so-called "modern" approach to scientifically studying the "true nature" of the human mind. Rather, our contemporary studies must yield to a humbler "postmodern" approach that privileges the construction of various perspectives for learning about aspects of our minds that interest us.

In psychotherapy we seek to alter minds. We approach this task with trepidation because, in dabbling with an infinity of possibilities, we can hardly know which way to turn, what perspectives we can construct that will help us learn about what we would most like to learn about. Where do we start? What exactly would we like to know about our clients and ourselves? And why?

We begin with the assumption that human beings are born genetically endowed with a complex brain and central nervous system. We further assume that this human central nervous system grows in complexity over time due to inborn natural processes as well as through its interactions with the physical and socio-cultural environment. We also assume that earlier developments—both phylogenetically and ontogenetically—provide basic templates for guiding later developments, although spontaneously emergent alterations also occur. A final assumption would be that many trajectories of human mental development might be defined for study, but none are of greater interest to human life than how human relationship possibilities are able to expand in complexity and consciousness over time. This last assumption raises the questions as to how expanding relational possibilities can become stopped, blocked, arrested, or repressed. And under what conditions can relational expansion be resumed? That is, how can we understand what the mind-altering process of psychotherapy might be about? With these questions in mind and as an introduction to seven Relational Listening Perspectives that psychotherapists tend to find useful, let me tell you a little story that illustrates the growth of human relatedness possibilities.

Jaden Encounters Alexandria

My eight-year-old grandson Jaden is an only child raised in a warm and relationally rich environment with a large family of parents, grandparents, aunts, uncles, cousins, and friends. But he has had no direct experience with babies. Since he is at an age of being invested in building talents and skills, I wanted to introduce him to four-month-old Alexandria, a new baby of some friends of mine. She too is an only child with a warm and relationally rich set of parents and extended family. We bring carry-out Chinese food to our visit as a contribution to the complexities of family life with a new baby.

When we arrive, Alexandria has just woken up from a nap and is propped up with blankets and soft toys in her car seat. Her parents have placed her seat on the area rug in the center of the room for Jaden's benefit. He has been looking forward to meeting Alexandria and sets immediately to work! Seated cross-legged on the floor in front of her he moves in close saying hello in as many ways as he can muster. She sees him but doesn't show much interest at first—after all, she has just woken up from a nap. But Jaden is not perturbed. He is set on finding her. He tries moving his head from side to side, clapping his hands, making funny noises, and at last waving various toys and rattles in front of her. She slowly takes him in, not quite sure what to make of all of this activity since she has not had exposure to children in her short four months of life. It occurs to Jaden to stick out his tongue and bingo—she sticks out her tongue in response and the relationship begins!

I wish I had taken notes. But notetaking would undoubtedly have interfered with the rich and amazing spontaneity that occurred before our grownup eyes. It is rapid-fire back and forth. He covers his eyes and she blinks. He makes clicking noises and she clicks too. When she looks away Jaden is mildly perturbed. But he seems to understand that she is taking things in, trying to make sense of what is happening. At first he tries to force her attention back to the interaction but then he backs off and waits for her to return her attention on her own and the games begin again. When it gets a little boring Jaden's attention strays but she wildly waves her arms and loudly vocalizes to draw him back. It is then time for a bottle break and Chinese food and afterwards more games starting with tongue protrusions. They have each found a new friend and they are obviously happy about it before it is time for bath and bed. Jaden is entranced with the whole set of bath and bedtime rituals and with her father softly humming Alexandria to sleep.

Logistics make it difficult to get Jaden and Alexandria together more than every couple of months. But each time on the way to visit Jaden speculates about what she might be up to now. Amazingly enough, every time she recognizes him the minute he walks through the door. She lights up eagerly ready to play. Each time there are new toys and new ways of her sitting up, vocalizing, and moving around. Jaden quickly enters into the new situation and adapts his interactive skills to fit the moment and her advancing relational capacities. He is excited and proud to be able to figure out how to connect with her in new ways each time we visit. Can she roll over now? Will she be crawling this time? Will she have words? What will her first words be? When will she be walking do you think? Each visit is a new adventure for both of them as they expand their relationship engagement. No, she isn't walking yet but did you see how fast she raced across the floor in her new little walker? Jaden crawls on the floor as fast as he can and waits for her to race behind him and catch up. Then he hides around the corner but she finds him in no time at all. She can now play new kinds of peekaboo and go after the ball when it is rolled across the room. Jaden is clearly pleased at how adept he is in figuring out new ways to engage her.

They have learned to play off of each other and they are happily excited about it. What will be next? We can expect more emotional mutual attunement and engagement—attachment style. Then later we can expect her showing off for him how well she can color and jump and throw the ball. Then they will begin sharing—having tea parties and picnics and passing the pretend cookies, sandwiches, tea, and juice back-and-forth. Family adventures will evolve in the doll house and new narratives in the puppet theater. Then come the board games, the ghost stories, and video game competitions. Only very much later will they be aware of what they are wearing and how their hair is combed when the other is coming to visit—what music each is listening to, what video games each is playing now, what each is posting on Facebook, and what kind of friends they each have. Thus goes the amazing human pageant of relational development! Jaden and Alexandria are off to a great start.

Even by eight years of age Jaden has already learned the crucial relational lesson: *if we want to engage somebody in a relationship, we must attune our engagement efforts to different developmental issues and capacities as they are being offered and experienced at that moment in that relationship.* His time with Alexandria suggests that he himself has already learned six of the seven essential relational complexity skills we will soon define and is ready for adolescence when it arrives. That is, he has already developed a strong sense of an independent self and how to fully engage another developing similar but different—separate self.

The specifics of how Jaden engages Alexandria are necessarily culture-bound, as every cultural orientation is imbued with its own symbols, values, rituals, and heroes that color each new phase of relational development.[3] But our human needs and capacities for relatedness—based as they are on human genetic determinants are essentially the same across cultures. And in human development they proceed from simple relational forms to more complex forms, regardless of culture.

_____
[3] Hedges, 2012a.

Tragically, Jaden, like the rest of us, as he moves into adolescence and young adulthood will largely lose track of the myriad subtleties of these valuable early relational learning experiences as he comes to defer to the strong socio-political-economic narratives and directives offered by literature, public and social media, and values available in this culture. That is, cultures teach us perceptions, narratives, and ways of being that highlight "the way things and people are or should be." So that, over time, it seems that we tend to gradually lose our sense of how to negotiate the many carefully nuanced understandings of relational possibilities that we once knew as young children. This loss of early emotional/relational sensitivities at this point in history seems to be greater for the male-gendered cultural versions of identity than for the female-gendered versions—at least in most cultures.

This book examines seven distinctly different perspectives for experiencing, imagining, and entering into the intimacies of relational life with other human beings—regardless of culture. We will consider seven Relational Listening Perspectives that have evolved over more than a century of psychological and psychoanalytic study. We will then apply them to understanding the personally constructed inner worlds of each of us. As a psychologist-psychoanalyst I have a special interest in thinking through how to use these seven Relational Listening Perspectives in psychoanalytically-oriented psychotherapy. But these perspectives are equally as important for enhancing relatedness in other therapies and growth-producing endeavors, as well as in our everyday intimate relationships.

The meanings and importance of these seven perspectives can perhaps best be understood by briefly considering how they have emerged over historical time.

A Historical Note:
Sigmund Freud's Stroke of Genius

Freud's singular stroke of genius can be simply stated: *When we engage with someone in an emotionally intimate relationship, the deep unconscious emotional/relational habits of both participants become interpersonally engaged and enacted thereby making them potentially available for notice, discussion, transformation, and expansion.* In my view, all other wisdom regarding psychological growth and transformation put forward since the beginning of psychological time pales in light of this central seminal insight.

The story of the origin of this insight begins in 1885 when the young neurologist Sigmund Freud visits the famed physician Jean-Martin Charcot in Paris to observe his work with patients believed to have neurological diseases. Charcot demonstrates that with certain "hysterical" patients under hypnosis the crippled can be made to walk, paralyzed hands can be made to work, and blindness can be converted to sight. Freud concludes from these observations that these seemingly neurological conditions must have underlying or unconscious *psychological* causes. Further, the stories that patients tell under hypnosis make clear to Freud that their physical symptoms are profoundly related to troubling interpersonal relationships in the patients' lives.

Following a decade of clinical research and a series of stimulating weekend conversations in Berlin with his friend and colleague Dr. Wilhelm Fleiss, Freud in 1895 scribbles out on the train returning to Vienna from Berlin a draft that is later to become known as "A Project for a Scientific Psychology" (1895).

In attempting to come to grips with the nature of unconscious emotional habits Freud's "Project" envisions a human neurological system that (1) reaches into the environment to perceive and manipulate external realities; that (2) reaches into the body to perceive and manipulate internal realities; and that (3) integrates through a central organizing sense of "I" the two sets of perceptions and abilities into a memory system moving the child forward into human life. Freud comes to believe that the most important features in the human environment are emotionally significant human relationships. That the human brain and the sense of "I" actually develop according to relationship possibilities that are and are not available to the growing child. Said differently, *Freud came to believe that human growth involves relationship experiences that the child is able to create with people in the outside world that can connect with the physiological and emotional life within*—as we saw happening with Jaden and little Alexandria earlier.

As a child's experiences expand, working memory establishes a series of expectations and habits based on the relational environment that child has been born into. As the child grows, different patterns of relational complexity become established in what one might describe as *increasingly complex relational possibilities*. In average expectable development these successively more complex layerings of relational achievement become more or less comfortably integrated and re-integrated. But in conditions that Freud first studied as "neurosis", various relational possibility patterns are seen as somehow unconsciously blocked or stuck in time—i.e., "repressed."

24

Modern neurological knowledge confirms the essentials of Freud's 1895 model of neurological functioning. [4] The central insight regarding internalized relational expectations that Freud established is by now well accepted and understood. But the profound implications of how these internalized patterns of relational expectation limit human growth and how these patterns can later be relationally transformed in order to allow maturational resumption, are seldom fully appreciated. That is, Freud's central discovery and the subsequently accumulated knowledge of over a century of clinical research points to the ways that emotionally intense intimate relationships can be engaged in order for limiting patterns of relatedness to become enacted, processed, and transformed. In other words, *Freud's enduring contribution is not about the nature of mind, mental development, or mental health per se, but rather about how to engage in an intimate relationship in which limiting emotional relatedness patterns brought forth from the pasts of both participants can become expressed, enacted, and expanded in the present interpersonal setting.*

Allow me to clarify the above with the following thoughts. Freud labeled his research tool and healing art "psychoanalysis", borrowing a metaphor from 19th-century chemistry in which "analysis" meant to treat a complex compound in such a way as to break it into its component elements. Freud believed that by establishing an intimate, confidential relationship and treating the neuroses with hypnosis and later with free association and interpretation, that he could cause neurotic complexes (early unconscious relational blocks) to become conscious and, in the

---

[4] Ginot, 2015; Damasio, 1994, 1999, 2003, 2010; LeDoux, 1996, 2002; Porges, 2011; McGilchrist, 2010.

process, to break down into their component elements so that consciousness could resume its natural or normal expansion. That is, reasoning that the elemental instinctual or life forces an infant brings into the world—anabolism (building up) and catabolism (breaking down)—are subjected to adaptive learning during the course of early development, Freud's therapeutic technique sought to bring into expression and then through intimate relating to break down, analyze, or destroy those learned but inhibiting or limiting (neurotic) patterns so that ordinary, expectable emotional growth could resume its natural expanding course.

We now have a history of more than a century of psychological practitioners devising various analytic theories and techniques aimed at promoting this breaking down or analytic process. Although Freud's general understandings have been adopted by and adapted to many kinds of psychotherapy, it is this essential systematic elucidation and breakdown process that psychoanalytic psychotherapies aim to accomplish but is only dimly understood outside the profession and even frequently misunderstood within the profession.

In brain language, adaptive learning builds synaptic linkages. Most psychotherapies, along with educational, meditational and other physical and spiritual or mindfulness practices especially championed by interpersonal neurobiologists focus on the *building up* and expansion through neuroplasticity processes of positive neuronal connections. Conversely, *psychoanalytic therapies aim to bring into relational focus expressive, enactive, and directive processes that will permit a breaking down of ineffective or inefficient relational habits and patterns—thus releasing the blocked or bound up energies to pursue new expanded relational possibilities.*

For example, Interpersonal Neurobiologist Daniel Siegel (1999, 2007, 2010, 2012) indeed acknowledges the dark side of developmental processes particularly in his studies of insecure attachments and trauma using the label "shadows of the synapses" but then moves on to champion the cultivation of mindfulness and neuroplasticity. In contrast, a century of psychoanalytic study has placed at center stage an array of developmentally determined relational habits that are seen as gravely limiting to creative and fulfilling human life. Stated differently, most psychotherapies, educational techniques, and interpersonal neurobiology aim at building up adaptive relational responses through various goal-oriented and/or mindfulness techniques relying on adaptive learning and neuroplasticity. In contrast, psychoanalytically-oriented psychotherapies since Freud aim at bringing to expressive enactment in the therapeutic relationship seriously limiting interpersonal relatedness habits and modes so that they can become known, broken down, worked through, and transformed or expanded.

Perspectives for Generating
Personal and Interpersonal Knowledge

In my book *Listening Perspectives in Psychotherapy* (1983/2003, I proposed for that time a radical and far-reaching shift in orientation for thinking about the ways that therapists can come to know things—a shift which has yet to be widely appreciated. I cite philosopher Ludwig Wittgenstein (1953) as pointing out that the form for our human beliefs and propositions is generally, "This is the way things are." But in fact this way that we habitually formulate things as "true" is invariably merely a lens or frame through which we perceive things—not whatever unknown and unknowable "truths or realities" the things in themselves might have. That is, according to Wittgenstein, realities are much too complex to pin down for all time so we develop lenses and frames that provisionally suit various purposes.

Thus, while theories or models of human nature may provide us with a sense of security about what we think we know, when we actually encounter another human being we need to realize that person's internal world is entirely unique and totally unknown and in many ways forever unknowable to us. True, common sense, cultural narratives, and psychological science may provide some cultural-specific generalized dimensions of human experience for us to consider, but the personal inner world of the living, breathing individual human being before us defies such generalized understandings. In other words, *whatever it is we do in psychodynamic therapy cannot possibly be conceived as fully or deeply understanding another human being.*

So what are we doing with all of our insightful ideas, brilliant inquiries, and wise interpretations? I say, we are merely stirring the soup! That what is said to us and the ways we are related to has various impacts on us which we register and respond to in the best ways we know how in the moment—just as we saw young Jaden doing earlier with Alexandria. In our fumbling efforts it is not that we are stupid or that we have not been well-trained in our discipline, but rather that, as Freud and many others since have taught us, the purpose of our training is to enable us to engage in a relationship in which long-standing deep unconscious relational habits on both sides become enacted, discovered, discussed, transformed, and expanded.

In the words of the interpersonal psychoanalyst Edgar Levenson (1972, 1983, 2017), in psychotherapy we first set up the arrangements for our meetings. Second, through detailed inquiry or free association we gather the details and themes of the person's life, and third we discover how we are unconsciously mutually enacting these same themes in the here-and-now of the therapeutic relationship. The process of extended inquiry, discovery, and discussion outlined in this simple algorithm carries us away from ineffective and inefficient relational habits toward increasingly expanded consciousness and relational capacities.

Out of all of these complex and, at times, dismaying considerations arises the notion of formulating "Relational Listening Perspectives"—i.e., of defining ways of being emotionally and interactively present so as to encourage the emergence of inhibiting relational habits into the current interactive moment. In other words, if we cannot possibly know the "true nature" of another human mind, and if formulating preset models of the mind against which to compare individual experience runs the risk of biasing the listening/interactive experience, what stance can we possibly take in a therapeutic relationship that allows us to move forward while honoring our necessarily perennial uncertainty? My answer to this question as early as 1983 was by the construction of Relational Listening Perspectives. I used then, as I always have, the term "listening" in the broadest possible sense—meaning being emotionally present, paying close attention, interacting, processing, and responding in as many relevant ways as humanly possible. Let Jaden be our mentor!

The Relational Listening Perspectives, simply defined as a series of increasingly complex relational possibilities, make no particular assumptions about the nature or content of human mind except that human minds develop and expand in a relational context. In my 1983 research covering a century of psychoanalytic studies, four main watersheds of relational complexity emerged. Some years later when I studied Listening Perspectives from the standpoint of relational fears and the ways they manifest in our bodies, those four watersheds became divided into seven distinctly different kinds of relational experience and fear.[5] In the current *Handbook* I follow up the seven relational fears with seven corresponding perspectives for ways of reaching out for relational connectedness that are as culture- and gender-resonant as possible. Any particular number of defined perspectives is, of course, arbitrary, but these seven are what have emerged from my research and clinical studies.

Since the publication of *Listening Perspectives in Psychotherapy*, the concept of perspectives has become fairly popular in psychoanalytic parlance. I am seldom credited with any priority of thought—I think because most people still do not grasp the radical vision of my book. There are, of course, many standpoints from which anything can be considered and people get that. But that fact was by no means the full thrust of my book. *Using Relational Listening Perspectives as I conceived them requires a total re-orientation of one's therapeutic mindset*—a radically revised sense of how we come to know about and resonate with significant mental events and processes in ourselves, our clients and our emotionally significant others.

Allow me to briefly explain my notion of Relational Listening Perspectives by using the computer metaphor of hardware and

---

[5] See Hedges, 2012b, 2013.

software. We might consider human beings as endowed with incredible genetic and constitutional hardware. Also, the human socio/cultural/economic/linguistic environment as it has evolved over millions of years acts as part of the human hardware system. But the individual zygote—fetus—infant—child—adolescent—adult is impacted minute by minute throughout his or her life by idiosyncratic environmental forces such that virtually all mental content is totally unique—however much it may be formatted into common language and cultural features learned along the way. No general theories of mind will help us bring forth the uniqueness of the subjective worlds of therapist and client and the intersubjective/interactive field they co-create.

If the therapeutic consciousness-expansion goal of Levenson's three step algorithm is to be realized then *the unique themes, patternings, modes, and habits of relatedness of both participants must have an opportunity to emerge in fullness in the here and now relationship experience.* That is, *in the course of growing up at all levels of relational complexity development we each ran into barriers of various sorts leaving myriad memory traces and inhibitions.* The relational adventure of psychotherapy is one of coming to *re-experience* these habits and relational modes and how they operate beneath awareness in the here-and-now of life and psychotherapy. Simply talking about them will be insufficient for significant life-changing expansions. Our relational habits and modes must be an enacted, lived in relationship and brought into mutually engaged consciousness.

It follows that the questions arising for the therapist are: "How can I be of some use to this person wishing to expand her consciousness?" And after the therapy gets going, "What's going on here, anyway?", "Where is our relationship taking us?", and finally, "What is there to do about all of this?"

My answer to these questions is simply, "Pay close attention and involve yourself in the relationship according to Levenson's three-part algorithm." Whatever knowledge is to be gained will be a product of two people collaborating, enacting, and expanding their joint consciousness. Recall that "consciousness" is from the Greek words meaning "knowing together." In other words, what we are searching for in the psychotherapy encounter is the ongoing mutual construction or re-construction of life narratives as spoken and enacted in the here-and-now of relating. Stated negatively, we are *not* looking for any diagnostic or developmental categories or models or any character structures, content, or processes that occupy complex realms of mental structures or mechanisms, but rather personal expressions of life relational experiences and revelations of how those experiences are alive and well in our present relationships including the therapeutic relationship.

The next questions: how exactly are the Relational Listening Perspectives best formulated? And how exactly is one to make use of them? In Part Two I provide a schematic overview of the Relational Listening Perspectives. In Part Three I flesh out the seven experiences of reaching out and their corresponding fears. And in Part Four I address psychotherapy alteration, expansion, and transformation. A *Handbook* cannot possibly cover the extensive research and clinical experiences that have given rise to these ways of working, but here you will get a fair introduction and an overview of our 45-year project.

Aside on Therapeutic Change:
Dialogue, Intersubjectivity, and the Present Moment

As a brief prologue to the later Part Four that will deal with psychotherapeutic change, I would like to reiterate that the Relational Listening Perspectives approach is *not* an attempt to theorize on the nature of mind, of human development, or of psychotherapy. Rather, it offers a series of practical ways that we can position ourselves as listeners —in the broadest possible sense—*in order to resonate deeply with the inner relational worlds of our clients and ourselves with the general expectation of mutual expansion and transformation.* Again, let Jaden and Alexandria be our guides!

In considering the nature of psychological change and summarizing a century of psychoanalytic theorizing and practice from classic Freud through the carefully defined Ego Psychology of Anna Freud and Heinz Hartmann, to the numerous contemporary theoreticians and practitioners of Intersubjective psychotherapies, psychologist-psychoanalyst Roy Schafer (1995) outlines the seeds and forerunners to the contemporary relational approaches pointing out that for some time now "dialogue and intersubjectivity have been moving to the center of psychoanalytic interest.... To put it briefly, 'dialogue' conveys the idea that *in the course of [psychoanalytic psychotherapies] the understandings and the changes that take place can only come about through an evolving dialogue between analyst and analysand; in other words, the definition and reshaping of the self and other only take place in verbal and nonverbal dialogue.* And 'intersubjectivity' conveys the embeddedness of each person's cognitive and emotional position and his or her dialogic orientation in so-called real or imagined relations with others (emphasis added)." Schaefer holds that it has always been intuited and vaguely understood that the agent of change in psychoanalytically oriented psychotherapy is the dialogic nature and intersubjective reach of the therapeutic relationship itself.

The question of how exactly to consider psychological change from the standpoint of two-person psychology has been tossed about by many theoreticians and clinicians for some time now.[6] Especially prominent participants in this widespread conversation have been the infant researchers and psychoanalytic scholars in the Boston Change Process Study Group (2007). After years of study and intense research they have generally concluded that *change processes occur between two or more people in a given moment in time.*

The clearest statement of the human change process emanating from that group comes from infant researcher Daniel Stern. In his book *The Present Moment* (2004), Stern's wide-ranging studies reveal that the basic unit of human experience—the present moment—lasts eight to 16 seconds—the time for a phrase in language, music, and dance. Like the illustrations in our Psychology101 text that demonstrated that we do not see in sweeping panorama but rather in momentary points of visual fixation, so too our sense of living an ongoing life panoramic experience is derived from our brain's putting seamlessly together a series of eight to 16 second "present moments."

---

[6] See, for example, Bollas, 1987; Aron, 1996; Mitchell, 1988; and Benjamin, 1988.

What are the implications of these findings for relational psychotherapy?

According to Stern, in ongoing intimate relationships ordinary "present moments" often move toward special "now moments" that threaten the status quo of the relationship and the intersubjective field as it has been mutually created and accepted up until then. That is, a relationship can be developing quietly in a series of present moments that lead up to some rift or rupture, some misunderstanding, divergence of views, or other interpersonal disjunction. These emotionally intense "now moments" represent a relationship crisis that needs resolution. The resolution of the relationship crisis occurs in what Stern calls "a moment of meeting...an authentic and well-fitted response to the crisis created by the now moment. The 'moment of meeting' implicitly reorganizes the intersubjective field so that it becomes more coherent, and the two people sense an opening up of the relationship, which permits them to explore new areas together implicitly or explicitly" (pp. 219-220).

For example, an intimately relating couple moves forward connecting in a series of "present moments" toward a moment of difference or disjunction causing a relationship crisis—a "now moment" that is, an emotionally charged rift. If two are then successful in creating a "meeting of minds", new understanding and new intimacy is created that is part of the relationship-building journey. If not, repeated unresolved crises lead to relationship disruption, to stalemates, to distancing, to divorce.

Stern's moment-by-moment analysis of what is going on in relationships that promote change permits us to consider that whatever motivational systems for reaching out to another may be operating, they are immediate and intense in intimate relationships. We know how difficult it can be for us to live in and to cultivate on an ongoing basis transformative present moments and moments of meeting in our intimate relationships. The lesson is clear—whatever importantly motivates us in relationships is operating in the here-and-now present moment and deserves our mutual attention and focus. If we cannot live together in the present moment our relationships are dragged down by the past or weighed by anxieties about the future—neither of which we can do anything about at the moment. *The clear conclusion is that lasting meaningful change is only possible through an emotionally charged present relationship that is imbued with mutual concern and intention.* This psychological truth has recently been heavily underscored by advances in our understanding of the neurological unconscious.[7]

---

[7] Ginot, 2015; Damasio, 1994, 1999, 2003, 2010; LeDoux, 1996, 2002; McGilchrist, 2010.

Part Two

A SCHEMATIC OVERVIEW OF RELATIONAL LISTENING PERSPECTIVES

Getting a Panoramic View

Flying over Manhattan, Toronto, Paris, Shanghai, or Orange County I find particularly thrilling because it allows me to see everything in breathtaking panorama, to see all of the places I know or have visited on the ground from an angle that puts them all together in a newly comprehensible way. On the other hand, viewing abstract ideas in a schematic overview can sometimes become tedious and seemingly over-intellectualized unless one seeks to grasp the total panorama and tries to relate *personally* to the schema being presented. Since the Relational Listening Perspective approach has been a forty-five-year project contributed to by many people and continuously expanding, a *Handbook* and a schematic overview may help pull things together for you or at least serve to get you started on a different, hopefully panoramic, way of thinking about relationships, especially the therapeutic one. What follows are the bare bones of Relational Listening Perspectives. In Parts Three and Four I will flesh out the ways these perspectives can be useful in forging ahead on a therapeutic adventure.

Listening Perspectives:
Frames for Understanding Relational Experience

The Listening Perspectives approach as I have defined it and others have used, adapted, and expanded it, aids *in framing* for therapeutic understanding different qualities of *internalized* interpersonal relatedness experience as they arise in the here-and-now cognitive-emotional-motivational matrix of the therapeutic relationship. The Relational Listening Perspectives approach further encourages us *to formulate* our work in terms of theories that enhance listening and speaking possibilities within a living, breathing, here-and-now relationship, rather than theories that seek to reify or personify mental processes or to capture the true nature of the human mind as objectively defined and viewed in isolation.

The Relational Listening Perspectives that follow are based on developmental *metaphors* of how a growing child potentially engages and is engaged by emotionally significant others in interpersonal interactions that build internal habits, modes, or patterns of relational expectation and competence. Relational Listening Perspectives thus formed are *not* intended to represent a developmental schema *per se*, but rather to identify a general array of increasingly complex relatedness possibilities lived out each day by all people.

Below you will find the original four perspectives—The Organizing, Symbiotic, Selfother, and Independence Experiences interspersed with elaborations of the seven interpersonal relatedness perspectives and their corresponding relational fears.

Overview of the Relatedness Listening Perspectives[8]

I. THE ORGANIZING EXPERIENCE

Infants require certain forms of connection and interconnection in order to remain psychologically alert and enlivened to themselves and to others. In their early relatedness they are busy "organizing" physical and mental channels of connection—first to mother's body, later to her mind, and then to the minds of others—for nurturance, stimulation, evacuation, and soothing. Framing organizing patterns for analysis entails studying how two people approach to make connections and then turn away, veer off, rupture, or dissipate the intensity of the connections. The Organizing Experience is metaphorically conceptualized as extending from 4 months before birth to 4 months after birth.[9]

—Perspective 1—

Reaching Out to Have Our Needs Met

Infants are programed genetically in many ways to reach out into the human environment for stimulation, nurturance, soothing, and evacuation. When an infant repeatedly reaches out in whatever ways possible and the environment is unresponsive, the infant's reaching slumps and withers—thus forming an internalized habit of painful inhibition and withdrawal.

---

[8] In my books on relational fears (2012b, 2013b) I credit bioenergetics analysts Virginia Wink Hilton and Robert Hilton for helping me formulate the way psychological experiences of fear "hook into" the body.

[9] The Organizing Experience (often thought of in terms of psychosis, schizophrenia, bipolar, autistic spectrum, and major depressive and anxiety disorders) is developed especially in Hedges, 1994a, 1994c, 2000b, 2013c.

The First Relational Experience Fear

We dread reaching out and finding nobody there to respond to our needs. We fear being ignored, being left alone, and being seen as unimportant. We feel the world does not respond to our needs. So what's the use?[10]

—Perspective 2—

Reaching Out to Make Connections

Infants are genetically programmed for bonding through mutual affective regulation with their caregivers. When they reach out and experience rejection or injury they quickly learn to "never reach that way again."

The Second Relational Experience Fear

Because of frightening and painful experiences in the past, connecting emotionally and intimately with others feels dangerous and potentially hurtful. Our painful life experiences have left us feeling that the world is not a safe place. We fear injury so we withdraw from connections.

II. THE SYMBIOTIC EXPERIENCE

Toddlers are busy learning how to make emotional relationships (both good and bad) work for them. They experience a sense of merger and reciprocity with their primary caregivers, thus establishing many knee-jerk, automatic, characterological, and role-reversible patterns or scenarios of relatedness. Framing the symbiotic bonding or attachment relatedness scenarios entails noting how each person characteristically engages the other emotionally and how interactive scenarios evolve from two

---

[10] The Seven Deadly Fears are the subject of Hedges 2012b, 2013b, 2015.

subjectively-formed sets of internalized self-and-other interaction patterns. The symbiotic attachment experience is *metaphorically* conceptualized as spanning from 4 to 24 months—peaking at 18 months.[11]

—*Perspective 3*—
Reaching Out to Form Attachments

Attachment or bonding through processes of mutual affect regulation is a fundamental biological drive. The self and other bonding scenarios or dances established are life sustaining. Being unable to find one's bonding partner(s) is terrifying and disorienting.

The Third Relational Experience Fear

After having connected emotionally or bonded with someone in some way, we fear either being abandoned with our own needs or being swallowed up by the other person's needs. In either case we feel the world is not a safe or dependable place, that we live in danger of emotional abandonment. We may become clingy and dependent or we may become super-independent—or both.

—*Perspective 4*—
Reaching Out to Assert Ourselves

Human babies are not only pre-programed to emotionally resonate and attach but they are also pre-programmed to push away from the attachment figure in search of independence.[12] When

---

[11] The symbiotic experience (often thought of in terms of borderline and other character disorders, addictions, and eating disorders) is developed and expanded under the label "borderline personality organization" in Hedges, 1983/2003, 1992, 1996, 2013c, 2015.

[12] Slavin & Kleigman, 1997.

a child's attempts at self-assertion and separation-individuation are thwarted, frustration and anger usually results—anger that may get severely squelched.

The Fourth Relational Experience Fear

We have all experienced rejection and punishment for expressing ourselves in opposition to others. We come to fear asserting ourselves and our needs in relationships. We feel the world does not allow us to be truly ourselves. We may either cease putting ourselves out there altogether or we may assert ourselves with a demanding vengeance.

III. THE SELFOTHER EXPERIENCE

Three-year-olds are preoccupied with using the acceptance and approval of others for developing and enhancing self-definitions, self-skills, self-cohesion, and self-esteem. Their relatedness strivings use the admiring, confirming, and idealized responses of significant others to firm up their budding sense of self. Framing for analysis the selfother patterns used for affirming, confirming, and inspiring the self entails studying how the internalized mirroring, twinning, and idealizing patterns used in self-development in the pasts of both participants play out to enhance and limit the possibilities for mutual self-to-selfother resonance in the emerging interpersonal engagement. [13] The selfother experience is conceptualized *metaphorically* as extending from 24 to 36 months.[14,15]

---

[13] Kohut, 1971, 1977, 1984. Note that Kohut's original term is "selfobject."

[14] The Selfother perspective is developed strongly in Hedges 1983/2003 and expanded in 1992, 1996, 2013c, and 2015.

[15] The selfother experience is often thought of as Narcissistic Personality Disorder.

<u>Reaching Out for Recognition</u>

As separation-individuation proceeds, the growing child seeks recognition from others of his or her worthiness and competence as an independent self. At times the child needs affirmation; at times confirmation; and at times inspiration—all in order to develop a strong, healthy sense of independent selfhood.[16]

The Fifth Relational Experience Fear

When we do not get the acceptance and confirmation we need in relationships, we are left with a feeling of not being seen or recognized for who we really are. We may then fear we will not be affirmed or confirmed in our relationships. Or we may fear that others will only respect and love us if we are who they want us to be. We may work continuously to feel seen and recognized by others or we may give up in rage, humiliation or shame. Or we may deny the need through grandiosity.

IV. THE INDEPENDENCE EXPERIENCE

Four- and five-year-olds and beyond are dealing with triangular love-and-hate relationships and are moving toward more complex social relationships. In their relatedness they experience others as separate centers of initiative and themselves as independent agents in a socially cooperative and competitive environment. Framing the *internalized* patterns of independently interacting selves in both cooperative and competitive triangulations with real and fantasized third parties entails studying the emerging interaction patterns for evidence of repressive forces operating within each participant and

---

[16] Jessica Benjamin (1995, 1998) has developed ideas about the importance of recognition in the development of a cohesive self.

between the analytic couple that work to limit or spoil the full interactive potential. This experience is *metaphorically* conceptualized as extending from latency, though puberty and throughout life.[17]

—Perspective 6—
Reaching Out to Cooperate and Compete in Love and Hate

Once the child has established a firm sense of independence as a self she or he begins effectively interacting in triangular relationships in family and community with other selves recognized as fully separate and independent. Love triangles engender cooperation and competition that lead at times to a sense of success and at times to a sense of failure.

The Sixth Relational Experience Fear

When we have loved and lost or tried and failed, we may fear opening ourselves up to painful competitive experience again. When we have succeeded or won—possibly at someone else's expense—we may experience guilt or fear retaliation. Thus we learn to hold back in love and life, thereby not risking either failure or success. We may feel the world does not allow us to be fulfilled. Or we may feel guilty and afraid for feeling fulfilled.

—Perspective 7—
Reaching Out to Be Fully Alive

As children learn to experience love and hate as well as success and failure in triangular relationships, they are prepared for the

---

[17] The Independence Experience is developed extensively in Hedges, 1983/2003, but because it has been so widely studied elsewhere it is only briefly reviewed in Hedges, 1992, 1996, 2013b. The Independence Experience is often thought of as neurotic/normal.

cascade of triangular relationships that are met as one moves on to puberty and adolescence—toward creative group living.

The Seventh Relational Experience Fear

Our expansiveness, creative energy, and joy in our aliveness inevitably come into conflict with demands from family, work, religion, culture, and society. We come to believe that we must curtail our aliveness in order to be able to conform to the demands and expectations of the world we live in. We feel the world does not permit us to be fully, joyfully, and passionately alive. Rather than putting our whole selves out there with full energy and aliveness, we may throw in the towel, succumb to mediocre conformity, or fall into a living deadness.

Part Three

SUBJECTIVE EXPERIENCES THAT THE RELATIONAL LISTENING PERSPECTIVES CAN BE HELPFUL IN FRAMING

(Note: Each of the sections that follow is introduced with a text box repeating material from Part Two in order to keep each Experience and Fear in context.)

I. THE ORGANIZING EXPERIENCE: Infants require certain forms of connection and interconnection in order to remain psychologically alert and enlivened to themselves and to others. In their early relatedness they are busy "organizing" physical and mental channels of connection—first to mother's body, later to her mind and to the minds of others—for nurturance, stimulation, evacuation, and soothing. Framing organizing patterns for analysis entails studying how two people approach to make connections and then turn away, veer off, rupture, or dissipate the intensity of the connections. The Organizing Experience is metaphorically conceptualized as extending from 4 months before birth to 4 months after birth.

Reaching Out to Have Our Needs Met

Infants are programed genetically in many ways to reach out into the human environment for stimulation, nurturance, soothing, and evacuation. When an infant repeatedly reaches out in whatever ways possible and the environment is unresponsive, the infant's reaching slumps and withers—thus forming an internalized habit of painful inhibition and withdrawal

The First Relational Experience Fear: We dread reaching out and finding nobody there to respond to our needs. We fear being ignored, being left alone, and being seen as unimportant. We feel the world does not respond to our needs. So what's the use?

—Perspective 1—

The Experience of Reaching Out to Have Our Needs Met

We all experience periods in which nothing seems right. Our senses are momentarily dull. We don't feel quite ourselves. We don't feel clear headed. Our minds tend to wander. We can't get anything done. It's hard to reach out to friends and loved ones in our usual ways. We may find it difficult to get out of bed in the morning or to control our eating and drinking. Something definitely is bothering us but we cannot say exactly what. We are unable to enjoy ourselves or the people around us. We have little energy for life and nothing seems to perk us up.

Many people live most of their lives in continuous states of discontent, withdrawal, fatigue, lack of pleasure, discouragement, ill health, confusion, and unresponsiveness. It is the persistence of such states of mind and body that can point us toward studying the earliest of human fears—the Fear of Being Alone.

From the beginning of life the fetus expands and contracts—pulsating with its own rhythms in harmony with the life-rhythms which surround it, first with its mother and later with other caregivers. Without reciprocal rhythms the baby will die. Every mammal knows, "seek and cling to the warm, pulsating body or die." In delicate pulsations from its first heartbeat, the infant extends invisible tendrils to extract what it needs from the intrauterine environment to sustain life: bountiful nutrients, oxygen, warmth, and support. After birth the baby is on its own to suck for food, breathe for air, metabolize for heat, and build bones and muscles for support and mobility. It continues to reach to the environment for what it needs to survive. But, as research clearly shows, the human infant needs more than food, oxygen, and physical warmth: its reach needs to be met with positive affective connection and enlivening energy. This is what feeds and enhances the life force within.

When a mother or other primary caregiver is depressed, in shock, preoccupied with overwhelming problems, or when the spark of life in her is momentarily or perennially eclipsed or absent, then she cannot respond to her infant with optimal feeling, energy, emotional warmth and aliveness. Infant research now shows that this lack of responsiveness can even be experienced by the baby before birth in the womb and carried into later life as a body memory.[18]

---

[18] This work has been carried out by numerous researches, many of whom are member of the BCPG (2007) and especially Daniel Stern (1985, 2004).

It is impossible for a mother (or other caregiver) to be always present, lively, and totally responsive. It is also impossible for a mother to always have only positive feelings for her infant. For this reason, all of us have some experiences contained in our body's memory that "there's nobody there." This body memory becomes the basis for the lifelong Fear of Being Alone. The compelling image is one of being left out to die.

As infants we all depended on satisfying and stimulating responsiveness from our early caregivers to activate our aliveness. And there were times when, even under the best of child-rearing circumstances, the response was inadequate—times when we extended ourselves hoping to contact some essential movement or supply—times when the longed-for connection was not forthcoming. The result was some type of discouraged giving up. Not having contact when it was needed left us with the feeling that there was nobody there to meet our needs. "So what's the use?" This feeling then becomes the basis for a deep-seated fear of reaching out to people in our environment. We do not want to reach out again, only to find painfully that there is "nobody there."

Since the Fear of Being Alone is the most basic or primitive of human fears it is often the most difficult to experience directly in adult life. And because it is the farthest back in our personal history it may be the hardest to identify. Rather than feeling actually frightened, we may instead tend to be aware of a lack of zest and energy for life or for our important experiences and/or relationships. When we experience discouragement, we may feel dazed, confused, or collapsed. Most of the time we are able to exert a little energy and get things going again in relatively short order.

But we all have known painful, empty, fearful moments of feeling, "What's the use?"

A person whose early history included a profound lack of needed responsiveness may later suffer from chronic fatigue or frequently feel overwhelmed and stressed out. He or she may feel unnecessarily strained and anxious, or beset with physical symptoms which have no clear-cut medical or psychological explanations. The person may not be actually depressed in the usual sense of the word, but may feel discouraged, depleted, and/or lacking orientation or vitality. These qualities are often clearly reflected in a slumping or slouching body posture and a general physical appearance of fatigue, depletion, and collapse.

There are many ways in which the Fear of Being Alone is manifest in the lives of those around us. We note discouraged, weakened, and giving up kinds of responses in people who continue to eat, drink, or smoke in the face of medical information that these activities are endangering their lives. Many people with serious medical and psychological conditions fail to alter life-threatening habits, deny the seriousness of their condition, or simply give up when there are many options available for staying healthy and alive.

We may develop compensatory ways of assuring ourselves that we are not alone by manufacturing an exaggerated sense of liveliness. We may create a feeling of being fulfilled by filling our lives with stimulating activity. Or we may manufacture a feeling of being strong and together by developing an exaggerated sense of strength and wellbeing. But just underneath the surface of these ways of compensating lies a profound sense of emptiness, weakness, and aloneness. In order for vital change to take place, we must be willing to drop the compensatory behaviors long enough to face the fear that if we extend ourselves into the world—if we reach out—there will be nobody there. Through working with this fear, through facing it instead of avoiding it, and finally through taking the risk of reaching for what we need and desire, we can find ways to become more fulfilled and more truly alive.

—Perspective 2—
Reaching Out to Make Connections

Infants are genetically programmed for bonding through mutual affective regulation with their caregivers. When they reach out and experience rejection or injury they quickly learn to "never reach that way again."

The Second Relational Experience Fear: Because of frightening and painful experiences in the past, connecting emotionally and intimately with others feels dangerous and potentially hurtful. Our painful life experiences have left us feeling that the world is not a safe place. We fear injury so we withdraw from connections.

—Perspective 2—
The Experience of Reaching Out to Make Connections

We all know what it feels like to be moving forward in some personal or intimate situation when we suddenly feel ourselves quietly backpedaling. We find ourselves trying to avoid further emotional involvement with someone or trying to escape a relationship for reasons that are not altogether clear to us. We may be able to find fault with something about the situation or about the person involved. But deep inside we know there is something, some unnamable dread, some silent fear reflex pulling us back from making or maintaining contact. We know that fear often prevents us from pursuing a relationship that could turn out to be rewarding and satisfying. But we miss the opportunity—or we spoil it! We hear from others, "Just when I begin to get close, you bail out." Or, "There's something about you that is afraid of relationships." "Why do you avoid intimacy?"

By definition intimacy in relationships requires some degree of mutual openness and vulnerability. We may avoid certain kinds of intimate contact with others because, in our earliest history, we learned that human connections could be painful, and therefore dangerous and frightening. Like any frightened mammal we freeze, fight, or flee when danger threatens. Some people become rigid, immobilized, and frozen in face of intimate contact. Others characteristically pick fights or become irritable and critical. Still others simply run—either by literally leaving or by withdrawing their emotional availability. However we do it, we pull back because we do not dare risk the pain of connecting and being vulnerable and hurt again.

In reaching out and making connections with people around them babies often encounter painful experiences. Pain then becomes associated with the person who, from the infant's point of view, was present and therefore in some way was "responsible" for the pain. Or at least was responsible for not preventing it. Since babies are closely tied to caregivers, connection with people is almost always associated in one way or another with painful experiences in infancy.

A picture may clarify the early situation. Imagine an infant born with a thousand "invisible tendrils" reaching out in all directions into its human environment, actively seeking to latch onto sources of stimulation, pleasure, soothing, and safety. Many of these tendrils extend in pulsations that seek reciprocal responses to become enlivened. When they are not met, as we have already seen in the first Fear of Being Alone, the pulsating tendrils simply weaken or wither in a discouraged attitude of giving up.

But there are times when the reaching tendril is not only un-responded to in a timely and satisfying manner, but is actively discouraged, hurt, or shamed. The reaching is met with coldness, indifference, or hostility. In such cases the infant experiences the environment not as a world of pleasure and safety but as one of pain, hurt, and danger.

For the person whose earliest reaching for contact was a painful or even a traumatic experience, chronic anxiety, fearfulness, and even terror of connecting remain at the core of his or her being. Certain kinds of connections with others have come to be unconsciously feared and avoided at all cost. This unconscious avoidance of human contact can only work to set up obstacles which limit our relationship possibilities and stifle our passion for life. Chronic constrictions in our bodies, personalities, and relationships persist to tell a story about a time when our reaching out to connect with people whom we loved and trusted led to pain, fear, and withdrawal.

II. **THE SYMBIOTIC EXPERIENCE:** Toddlers are busy learning how to make emotional relationships (both good and bad) work for them. They experience a sense of merger and reciprocity with their primary caregivers, thus establishing many knee-jerk, automatic, characterological, and role-reversible patterns or scenarios of relatedness. Framing the symbiotic Bonding or attachment relatedness scenarios entails noting how each person characteristically engages the other and how interactive scenarios evolve from two subjectively-formed sets of internalized self-and-other interaction patterns. The symbiotic attachment experience is metaphorically conceptualized as spanning from 4 to 24 months-peaking at 18 months.

—Perspective 3—
Reaching Out to Form Attachments

Attachment or bonding through processes of mutual affect regulation is a fundamental biological drive. The self and other bonding scenarios or dances established are life sustaining. Being unable to find one's bonding partner(s) is terrifying and disorienting.

The Third Relational Experience Fear: After having connected emotionally or bonded with someone in some way, we fear either being abandoned with our own needs or being swallowed up by the other person's needs. In either case we feel the world is not a safe or dependable place, that we live in danger of emotional abandonment. We may become clingy and dependent or we may become super-independent—or both.

—Perspective 3—
The Experience of Reaching Out to Form Attachments

We experience The Fear of Being Abandoned after we have entered into a personal relationship and then find that the other person cannot or will not be there for us in the ways we had hoped for or expected. We all know how devastating abandonment can be. Early experiences of abandonment have left us with the (often unconscious) fear that important people in our lives will leave us, betray us, neglect us, turn away from us, or even turn against us. In fact, we are so afraid of being abandoned that we often remain in relationships that are unsatisfying or even abusive. We grudgingly do what others want, out of the fear that they will leave us if we don't conform to their wishes. We give in to sexual demands when that's not what we want at the time. We go out of our way to meet other people's needs at the expense of our own. We give care to others at times when we ourselves need to be cared for. But we end up feeling used, empty, unsatisfied, and resentful—sometimes even hating the person or persons we serve. Despite our best efforts, in the end we are no less afraid of being abandoned.

For some of us the Fear of Being Abandoned is expressed in the resistance to forming close relationships. Being abandoned seems inevitable, so therefore we don't even risk the pain by getting too close or caring too much. Or at the first sign of dissatisfaction from our partner we leave, rather than risk the pain of being left.

The Fear of Abandonment is so strong in childhood that infants and toddlers will learn to tolerate almost any situation, no matter how limiting or abusive, so as not to be abandoned. In marriages and other close relationships we often see people engaged in and tolerating all manner of painful scenarios because they are terrified of abandonment. Our most fundamental belief about relationships is that we must seek out scenarios that are familiar and avoid those that are unfamiliar. In familiar scenarios, no matter how unpleasant they may be, we do not so greatly fear abandonment as we do in the unfamiliar ones. But in new or unfamiliar interactions we are in alien territory and we fear that we are or may be abandoned. Because we seek the familiar and we avoid the unfamiliar, in time we find ourselves inevitably going after relationships and emotional interactions that are terrible for us—but familiar. We are compelled to seek out or to create longstanding and known relationship scenarios—no matter how self-abusive or self-depriving they may be—so that we will not feel the danger of abandonment! By the same token we pass up opportunities for new and exciting kinds of growth, enrichment, self-expansion, and love because in earliest childhood we became afraid of breathtaking and unfamiliar new experiences that raised for us the risk of emotional abandonment.

The particular scenarios for relating to others which we each learned in the first two or three years of life are extremely limited; first, because we formed them with only the mental capacity of a toddler, and second, because our experience at that time was limited to our own home environment and family. Yet these patterns of relating continue to work automatically (and detrimentally) in all of our significant relationships for the rest of our lives—unless we find ways to dismantle them.

For example, how often do we find ourselves inexplicably attracted to someone who is clearly wrong for us? Because of some unconscious attitudes which we don't understand, we find ourselves again and again drawn toward or clinging to relationships which are empty, non-satisfying, and self-destructive. Or conversely, we find ourselves fleeing from relationships that might realistically be wonderful for us. For what reason we ignore them we are not quite sure. We are often painfully aware that the relationship models which were set in motion early in life silently continue to govern our choices in ways that are clearly not in our best interests. We continue to project all-good or all-bad "split" or "black and white" expectations onto others.

We develop either hopeful, optimistic idealizations; or negative, critical devaluations about others which are not realistic. Such opinions are the products of our automatic patterns. Our personal world view regarding good and bad, black and white relationships dramatically colors how we perceive and relate to others. We notice there are times when we simply cannot sustain sensible mixed feelings toward others. Instead we lapse into unthinking extremes of positive and negative feeling and continue relating in a naive or judgmental way.

The Fear of Abandonment appears in our idealized expectations that others will forever be available to us in loving and supportive ways. Our Abandonment Fear likewise appears in our negative expectations that the world is not a dependable place and that others are useless, self-centered, and ruthless.

—Perspective 4—
Reaching Out to Assert Ourselves

Human babies are not only pre-programed to emotionally attach but they are also pre-programmed to push away from the attachment figure in search of independence. When a child's attempts at self-assertion and separation-individuation are thwarted anger usually results—anger that may get severely squelched.

The Fourth Relational Experience Fear: We have all experienced rejection and punishment for expressing ourselves in opposition to others. We come to fear asserting ourselves and our needs in relationships. We feel the world does not allow us to be truly ourselves. We may either cease putting ourselves out there altogether or we may assert ourselves with a demanding vengeance.

—Perspective 4—
The Symbiotic Reaching Out to Assert Ourselves

There are times in our lives when we experience enormous anxiety over the seemingly simple matter of speaking up for ourselves. We may find ourselves unable to express disagreement with the boss or to ask for a much-needed and well-deserved raise. In our personal relationships we are apt to be compliant and agreeable, at least on the surface. We may cheerfully go along with our partner's agenda, even when it is at odds with our own. Yet after a while we begin to feel more than slightly ripped-off. We become uncomfortably aware that resentment and even hostility are building up inside us. Yet the prospect of a confrontation is so disturbing that we continue to stuff down our negative feelings. We may even find ways to blame ourselves. This suppressed burden of resentment, anger, and negativity is likely to cause us to feel sluggish, listless, weighed down, and generally unhappy. Or it may make us uptight, flighty, and anxious. Yet we tend to keep on a happy face. We may or may not be aware that the state we are in is profoundly connected to the Fear of Self-Assertion. We fear really putting ourselves "out there" in a full, alive, and independent manner.

Charting an efficient and fulfilling course between our needs for interdependence and our needs for independence is a lifelong project for all of us. The ways in which a toddler first learns to consider and to negotiate between competing sources of control has lifelong implications for all emotional issues involving self-assertion, opposition, compromise, negotiation, and loss of self-control. The Fear of Self-Assertion appears in all relationships that require a balance of competing self-interests.

The Fear of Self-Assertion shows up in many moments when we feel hurt, put down, or cast aside because our self interests are at odds with the interests of someone else. A slight threat of loss of control in a present relationship may trigger a long-standing fear of becoming lost in a power struggle in which we are likely to be painfully overruled or forced to face a humiliating defeat. The demand of a significant other may catapult us into fears of being completely lost or submerged by someone else's needs. We may automatically comply with or rebel against this perceived demand based on the history of our fear reflex.

Over time we have evolved many unconscious ways of managing our Fear of Self-Assertion. We may become passive or passive-aggressive. This means that while seeming to be positive and agreeable on the surface, we express our assertiveness and negativity indirectly. It may appear in subtle criticisms, barbs, hostile actions, delays, forgetting, or lateness. We may "act out" our anger by withholding affection from those whom we love. Not being "in the mood" can be a negative refusal to comply. Or we may establish blind prejudices rather than struggle with conflict, uncertainty, or insecurity.

Often, people who are afraid to assert their negativity have long lists of silent grievances toward those close to them. Beneath a smiling, agreeable countenance, their body is a repository of resentments and anger. Sometimes this adds up to enormous rage. Because the rage doesn't get directly expressed but is experienced passively or gets turned back upon one's self, it may become transformed into depression and/or many kinds of physical symptoms.

It's easy to see how the Fear of Self-Assertion wreaks havoc in our relationships. A partner may think it's great to have a compliant mate who goes along with his agenda and rarely makes waves. But the person who does not assert her needs or wishes and who does not directly express her negativity is surely building up a storehouse of resentment, anger, and rage. When anger comes out indirectly or passive-aggressively there is never a real opportunity to clear the air in the relationship. Grievances may be carried silently for years. The weight of withheld negativity drags down and finally buries the positive feelings. The clearing, refreshing, and renewing of the atmosphere which follows the electrical storm of an angry exchange between two people is never allowed to happen.

The Fear of Self-Assertion frequently shows up to cause damaging problems in sexual relationships. In this arena both men and women are often anxious about asserting their preferences, expressing their discomforts, and particularly, revealing any negative responses for fear they will be shamed, abandoned, shunned, or rejected by their partners or even by judgmental parts of themselves. They may keep the hurt feelings to themselves. But they secretly harbor destructive resentment when they are unfulfilled, dissatisfied, or unhappy. The negative feelings are stockpiled and the person deludes herself that she feels safe. But the problem is that when negativity is withheld, the passion in the relationship dies.

The result is often that, rather than facing and expressing the negativity, one or the other person leaves, the relationship is dissolved for lack of good feelings, or the relationship remains forever stagnant and unfulfilled. Those involved miss the opportunity to experience a certain reality about feelings: Withheld negativity acts as a block or barrier to experiencing good and positive feelings—including passion, joy, and sexual desire. When negativity can be fully expressed and processed by two the barrier is removed and the good feelings and sexuality can flow once again.

Workable and rewarding relationships require that each person involved be ready and able to assert her or his self-interests—often in opposition to the self-interests of others. Equally important is each person's readiness and availability to receive expressions of negativity, opposition, and anger from the other so that two can negotiate a rich, fulfilling, and passionate relationship.

III. THE SELFOTHER EXPERIENCE

Three-year-olds are preoccupied with using the acceptance and approval of others for developing and enhancing self-definitions, self-skills, self-cohesion, and self-esteem. Their relatedness strivings use the admiring, confirming, and idealized responses of significant others to firm up their budding sense of self. Framing for analysis the selfother patterns used for affirming, confirming, and inspiring the self entails studying how the internalized mirroring, twinning, and idealizing patterns used in self-development in the pasts of both participants play out to enhance and limit the possibilities for mutual self-to-selfother resonance in the emerging interpersonal engagement. The selfother experience is conceptualized *metaphorically* as extending from 24 to 36 months.

Reaching Out for Recognition

As separation-individuation proceeds, the growing child seeks recognition from others of his or her worthiness and competence as an independent self. At times the child needs affirmation; at times confirmation; and at times inspiration—all in order to develop a strong, healthy sense of independent selfhood.

The Fifth Relational Fear: When we do not get the acceptance and confirmation we need in relationships, we are left with a feeling of not being seen or recognized for who we really are. We may then fear we will not be affirmed or confirmed in our relationships. Or we may fear that others will only respect and love us if we are who they want us to be. We may work continuously to feel seen and recognized by others or we may give up in rage, humiliation or shame. Or we may deny the need through grandiosity.

—*Perspective 5*—
The Selfother[19] Experience of Reaching Out for Recognition

How many times do we find ourselves looking for the right thing to wear for a special event, certain that we will feel out of place or not comfortable if we don't find it? Or we worry if our hair isn't quite right or if a blemish appears. Or if we don't have the right shoes. We can't seem to feel okay about ourselves if our appearance doesn't suit us.

Certain social situations make us feel very insecure and we worry that we won't say or do the right things or that we won't be

---

[19] See note 13.

interesting enough. Being in the presence of some people—particularly ones we consider important or prestigious—can make us absolutely tongue-tied. Or at times we find ourselves "name-dropping" or slipping in references to our accomplishments in order to feel worthwhile. In our work we put up a self-assured front, but inside we wonder when the axe will fall.

Sometimes we have an underlying, nightmarish feeling that someday someone will expose us for the inept, inadequate persons we really at some level believe ourselves to be. We feel phony or like impostors.

We find ourselves needing reassurance from our partners and friends that we are okay. Yet when we're given compliments about how we look, how we perform, or who we are, at times it doesn't seem to make a real difference. We can't quite believe it anyway. Or at least their positive feedback may not take away our discomfort completely. Why don't we more consistently feel better about ourselves?

In order to develop self-respect, self-esteem, and self-love and the talents and skills that depend on self-cohesiveness, it is essential that who we are and how we are is seen, appreciated, affirmed, and mirrored back to us in various ways by significant people around us. When we did not receive adequate acknowledgment of our developing personhood in our early years, we grew up with feelings of being insignificant or even valueless. We later live out our lives with an underlying Fear of Not Being Recognized.

Unfortunately, many problems can and do arise when three-year-olds strive to have their psychological selves mirrored and strengthened. For example, a child comes excitedly running into the house, "Mommy, Mommy, see what I found!" But instead of prizing the treasure or the treasure seeker, Mother or caregiver may show more concern for mud on the carpet, for mussed up hair, or for a shirttail hanging out. Cleanliness, order, and decorum are being valued more than an excited self-expression.

Frequently, significant others fail to reflect how wonderful the growing talents and skills of the young child really are. When the child proudly exhibits to her parents some new creation or performs a new trick on her tricycle, an insensitive parent may be indifferent to her efforts, or tell her how she could have done it better. Or when the child verbally expresses pride and pleasure in herself, she may be met with words like: "Don't toot your own horn so loud," "You're getting too big for your own britches," "Don't be so self-centered," or "Don't break your arm patting yourself on the back!"

We all need recognizing and acknowledging others from birth to death—important people in our lives who see us and affirm us for who we really are and who we are striving to be. We need people who are pleased with our accomplishments, who are proud to be connected to us. The need for personal acknowledgment through being affirmed, confirmed, and inspired is universal and lifelong. If our earliest self strivings are met with sufficient acknowledgment, we will then tend to feel comfortable being ourselves throughout our lives. We will feel safe turning to others for recognition! But if our developing self was not adequately acknowledged in that early and crucial era, we may have learned immature or incomplete ways of gaining acceptance and compensating for feeling unacceptable. Our old patterns tend to cause distress and pain in our adult lives.

And we find, much to our chagrin, that we are stuck in childish or simplistic ways of seeking acceptance.

If, when we turn to others in search of confirmation of ourselves, we feel shamed or humiliated for our selfishness or self-centeredness, then we lose our sense of self-esteem and self-cohesion. We may become frantic or driven in an attempt to regain our self-esteem. Essentially stuck in a three-year-old mold we clamor in one way or another, "See me, see me!" Instead of receiving acknowledgment, we may feel or actually be met with painful shaming and humiliation from inside or outside for needing reassurance.

Failure to feel acknowledged may, on the one hand, leave us with a perennial readiness to fly into narcissistic rage, to puff up with righteous indignation, or to seek revenge for feeling wronged. Our sense of entitlement says, "Nobody's going to rain on my parade!" Or, on the other hand, we may become afraid of being humiliated for what is actually a perfectly normal and healthy need to be seen as strong and acceptable. We may come to feel that it is somehow wrong to take pride in self-achievement. Or that we are likely to be seen as self-centered or selfish if we express pride or seek confirming responses from others. In these ways faulty recognition in childhood results in either an inflated or a deflated sense of self, creating in us a world view in which our self-esteem feels constantly threatened. In feeling chronically deflated or over-inflated we may find ourselves as adults spinning our wheels in an attempt to correct problems of self-esteem developed in early childhood.

IV. THE INDEPENDENCE EXPERIENCE: Four and five-year-olds are dealing with triangular love-and-hate relationships and are moving toward more complex social relationships. In their relatedness they experience others as separate centers of initiative and themselves as independent agents in a socially cooperative and competitive environment. Framing the internalized patterns of independently interacting selves in both cooperative and competitive triangulations with real and fantasized third parties entails studying the emerging interaction patterns for evidence of repressive forces operating within each participant and between the analytic couple that work to limit or spoil the full interactive potential. This experience is *metaphorically* conceptualized as extending from latency, though puberty and throughout life.

—Perspective 6—
Reaching Out to Cooperate and Compete in Love

Once the child has established a firm sense of independence as a self she or he begins effectively interacting in triangular relationships in family and community with other selves recognized as fully separate and independent. Love triangles engender cooperation and competition that lead at times to a sense of success and at times to a sense of failure.

The Sixth Relational Experience Fear: When we have loved and lost or tried and failed, we may fear opening ourselves up to painful competitive experience again. When we have succeeded or won—possibly at someone else's expense—we may experience guilt or fear retaliation. Thus we learn to hold back in love and life, thereby not risking either failure or success. We may feel the world does not allow us to be fulfilled. Or we may feel guilty and afraid for feeling fulfilled.

—Perspective 6—
The Independent Experience of Reaching Out to Cooperate and Compete in Love and Hate

The Fear of Failure and Success affects most people to one degree or another. It manifests in feelings of not measuring up, of not being as good as some other person, or in feelings of anxiety about not being able to function as well as needed or expected. We may experience the fear as deeply devastating and paralyzing. Or it may simply cause us troublesome anxiety that inhibits our effectiveness. The Fear of Failure may create such intense internal constrictions that we completely blow a job interview or fail a crucial exam. Or it may undermine our composure and confidence so that we are unable to put our best foot forward. It may result in mild to severe performance anxiety when we are about to introduce ourselves to a group, to give a speech, to participate in a competitive sports event, or to perform before others in any capacity whatsoever. The Fear of Failure may hold us back from pursuing a particular relationship. Or it may inhibit us in our social interactions in a variety of ways.

We tend to judge success and failure in terms of other people—how our efforts, skills, products, or creative efforts measure up or compete with standards set by those around us. To the extent that success and failure are about winning and losing they also involve cooperation and competition. In one way or another we compete with others in order to be successful, or, one could say, to be chosen or acknowledged as successful or as a winner. Even when we explicitly compete with ourselves, comparisons to others are inevitable. Telling ourselves it doesn't matter if we win or lose may be a great idea but it simply doesn't touch our deep-seated fear reflexes.

There are also many ways in which we are afraid to win. The Fear of Success may manifest in the feeling that "something dreadful will happen if I really do win." "I may be drastically punished in some way if I do make it to the top." Or, "If I succeed I will have to keep on succeeding." When competing for a special position, or in a sporting event, or even for a personal relationship, we may inexplicably undermine ourselves at some decisive moment, therefore assuring our loss. To reverse a well-known phrase, sometimes we may have a penchant for "snatching failure out of the jaws of success!"

Competition always occurs in the context of "triangular" relationships whether that fact is obvious to us or not in a given situation. For example, the triangle may be comprised of me, the person I desire, and my real or imagined rival. Or the triangle may be me, the job I want, and the other applicants. Or the triangle may be my product, the consumer, and other competing products. The third party may be silently operating in the background of my mind as a moral value, a cultural proscription, or a judgmental attitude.

Or the third party may be a belief about what I "ought" to do, or what I think is the "right" way.

It is in the nature of competition and triangular situations that someone wins and someone loses in relation to the desired person, criterion, recognition, or goal. Thus, our attitudes about winning and losing are connected to the ways we relate to all forms of cooperation and competition. Our Fear of Failure and Success thus has its roots in our earliest experiences of triangular relationships: Myself, my mother, and my father—or whatever threesomes were available when we were four or five years old when cooperative and competitive attitudes first developed.

Freud's (1924) classic formulations of the "Oedipus Complex" are as rich and provocative today as when he first wrote about them. Each well-developed child during this four- to seven-year-old period is likely to experience both intensely loving and intensely hating feelings at the same time toward each parent or emotionally significant other. This is in contrast to the earlier developmental tendency to alternate in our love between "all-good" and "all-bad" feelings. The four- to seven-year-old learns to experience ambivalence (mixed and contradictory feelings) towards others who are emotionally significant. Conflicts over the universally intense and contradictory feelings of love and hate in family relationships were first celebrated in the ancient Greek myth of Oedipus and were later immortalized in Sophocles' play *Oedipus Rex* and in Shakespeare's *Hamlet*.

The fear of emotional injury and personal failure in the face of being left out of an emotional triangle, or, conversely, the fear of being the unchallenged victor in a competitive triangular conflict, becomes structured into our inner world view of relationship attitudes in a variety of ways. In *Oedipus Rex*, the guilty hero punishes himself with blindness (repression) when he has to look honestly at the ways he has ruthlessly lived out his sexual and aggressive impulses in relation to his parents. Many people similarly choose to live with diminished awareness of their sexuality and aggression. Hamlet sacrifices his life in the process of living out his instincts—"To be or not to be, that is the question." His Ophelia chooses madness and death over the loss of her self when feeling caught in social demands. Many people choose illness or emotional deadness over the possibility of being fully and vibrantly alive to the internal conflicts and insecurities necessarily involved in experiencing their full energetic potentials in socially cooperative and competitive relationships.

Our competitive strivings for dominance in love and our murderous rage over competitive defeat and failure (or over incestuous success) are all likely to produce intense guilt and repression of feelings in a young child. Repression of loving and hating feelings means that we have cultivated a blindness to our very nature and produced a deadening of all of our passionate quests in life. Far from being simply a dusty old myth, the problem of guilt and the Oedipus triangle lives on as the problem which every well-developed five-year-old faces and somehow solves with various forms of repression—blinding him- or herself to the power of the life forces within and deadening the outward expression of the instincts with fear-avoidance habits. The blinding and deadening constrictions we each developed during this period of Oedipal or triangular strivings have left their mark on our bodies, on our personalities, our sexuality, and on our relationships.

—Perspective 7—
Reaching Out to Be Fully Alive

As children learn to experience love and hate as well as success and failure in triangular relationships, they are prepared for the cascade of triangular relationships that are met as one moves on to puberty and adolescence— toward creative group living.

The Seventh Relational Experience Fear: Our expansiveness, creative energy and joy in our aliveness inevitably come into conflict with demands from family, work, religion, culture, and society. We come to believe that we must curtail our aliveness in order to be able to conform to the demands and expectations of the world we live in. We feel the world does not permit us to be fully, joyfully, and passionately alive. Rather than putting our whole selves out there with full energy and aliveness, we may throw in the towel, succumb to mediocre conformity, or fall into a living deadness.

—Perspective 7—
The Independence Experience of Reaching Out to Be Fully Alive

The Fear of Being Fully Alive is a fear associated with group life. As a result of a lifetime of living in groups we have come to feel stifled and stymied by the expectations and demands of the social world around us. The minute we come under the influence of any particular group, we are immediately aware of how people in this group walk, talk, dress, think, move, and behave. Each group we encounter is identifiable by characteristic codes, behaviors, and beliefs—the standards of the group. But no matter how much we may identify with the beliefs and standards of a group, we know that we are, in our own way, different. We learn to suppress our differences, to pull in our opinions and beliefs when they are at odds with the prevailing group climate. We dread the clashes which are an inevitable part of group life. We fear the influence which powerful group pressures exert on us. And we learn that it is often best to hold ourselves back, to keep our feelings under control, to inhibit our expressiveness, and to keep our opinions to ourselves.

The results of this mass social inhibition which we all participate in are truly appalling. Every day we watch people go about their lives like zombies—hardly noticing that the sun is shining, that flowers are blooming, and that all of nature is singing! We forget that we are living, breathing beings with a capacity for love and happiness, joy and sorrow, anger and fear.

Too often we pass through the day feeling stultified by the many demands upon us. Too often we forget about ourselves and our need for vibrant health and success in living. Too often we ignore the ones we love and deprive ourselves of the sense of life and aliveness we truly deserve. Too often we fail to allow ourselves the sense of fulfillment that comes from feeling truly connected with nature and with others whom we love and care about. And too often our bodies are wooden, our smiles strained, our eyes dull, and our hearts heavy.

It is as if we have somehow chosen to die before it is our time! We have become infected by forms of living deadness that we feel in people all around us. Whether it's eating, drinking, working, shopping, or watching television, we are devoted to a life of escape—from what? Where did all of this numbness, this inhibition, this deadness, this need to escape life come from? How can we focus on the ways we unwittingly allow lifelessness to take us in? How can we release the habitual restrictions which limit our personalities? How can we release the chronic contractions that bind our bodies? And how can we overcome the needless inhibitions that exist in our relationships? How can we unburden ourselves of the terrible deadening sense of obligation we have toward everything and everyone? How can we prevent social influences from threatening our peace of mind and our general well-being? How can we keep from being pushed into rigid postures and life-restricting habits and practices?

As human beings we are currently in the midst of a major crisis in terms of how we are to think about and manage ourselves in an anxiety-producing social environment. We are bombarded virtually every moment of our waking day with potentially frightening and overwhelming stimulation that has powerful effects on us. It is easy for us to blame our fears on the media, Hollywood, corporate life, urban living, technological advances, environmental toxins, and modern life in general. But the fear of intrusive and controlling social influences has always been a daily part of human life. Certainly the frequency, intensity, and invasive qualities of fear-producing social stimulation have increased in recent years. And our vulnerability to tension and stress-related diseases has also increased, no doubt in part due to the stimulus bombardment we continuously experience.

Contractions in the body serve to pull living organisms back from strong and overwhelming forces in the environment which are perceived as dangerous or life threatening. For humans those over-stimulating and threatening forces tend to be associated with relationships with important people and social demands. We are not simply creatures living in a jungle waking up each day and responding to the world on the basis of instincts and behavioral conditioning. We carry with us an evolving inner world view with a set of beliefs and expectations that color our everyday experiences in complex ways. Our world views based upon early learned responses to fear in relationships determine to a great extent how we perceive and respond in later situations. All of the seven levels of relationship fear and the reflexive contractions we develop early in life leave lasting imprints on our personalities, on our bodies, and on our ways of responding in later relationships.

In our journey toward greater aliveness things come at us every day that are frightening, that we brace ourselves against. But we have for so long conditioned ourselves *not* to actually experience fear that we fail to notice how profoundly we are affected by powerful and intrusive social forces on a daily basis. Cultivating full aliveness implies developing a heightened sensitivity to all of the intrusive and disturbing group influences that impinge on us in the course of a day.

We do not give our best to others when we pull back short of what we could give—short of where we could reach if we made the effort. We tend to stop short of what we could be—dominated by a plague of irrational and unconscious fears masquerading as anxiety, tension, fatigue, stress, anger, illness, and depression. How many of us can name a single relationship in which we have been willing and able to give our all to its fulfillment, no matter how frightened we are of the intimacy and commitment involved? We are painfully aware of how we shortchange the ones we love—our partners, our children, our friends, and our work colleagues. Now we can begin to become aware of how our fear of Being Fully Alive shortchanges us!

Part Four

PSYCHOTHERAPEUTIC ALTERATIONS, EXPANSIONS, AND TRANSFORMATIONS

I. THERAPY WITH THE ORGANIZING EXPERIENCE

The Developmental Thrust

Whenever the organizing experience is in play in the therapeutic relationship—whether with a person who lives a pervasive organizing experience or with a person who is living only momentary pockets of organizing experience—*the most important feature for observation is the movement toward connection and engagement and the subsequent disconnection from that engagement or potential engagement.* That is, the developmental thrust of an infant in the months immediately before and after birth is one of searching for merger with the maternal body and mind for nurturance, soothing, stimulation, and evacuation. In Donald Winnicott's (1949) words, the baby's task is "going on being." The needed environmental response Winnicott (1971) called "primary maternal preoccupation." But things can and do go wrong with this primary thrust toward merger connection—from toxemia in pregnancy, alcohol fetal syndrome, genetic and constitutional disturbances, incubators, adoptions at birth, maternal and family difficulties, insanity in the environment, and numerous other uncontrollable sociopolitical and economic intrusions.

Since perfect parental responsiveness is never possible, we understand that all babies experience traumas of one sort or another—to a greater or less degree. And that the impact of those traumas necessarily gives rise to internalized expectations of later relational traumas of a similar type.[20]

As listeners we can imagine that a continuum of potentially faulty or traumatic disconnections or ruptures can be experienced ranging from a total absence of response that produces lethargy, withering, and withdrawal to an intrusive or hurtful response that produces severe body constrictions of various types. Either way the questing mind collapses and the message "never reach that way again" becomes emblazoned on the neurological system. This will mean that in later relational encounters which the mind/brain experiences as similar, a primitive withdrawal or constrictive response of a similar nature is likely to result.

The Transference

All mammals are genetically programmed to search for the warm body or die. To me this accounts for why so many primitively organized clients search out trust relationships that they invest with hope. But no sooner than trust begins to build so that the person is encouraged to reach out for an enlivening connection than the impact of the traumas of the past resurface in the relationship to rupture any possibility of gaining or sustaining that connection.

---

[20] Hedges, 2015.

This connecting-disconnecting process can be readily observed in the micro process of an hour when there seems to be some movement towards connection which is then followed by some kind of disconnecting move. It can also be tracked on a macro level between sessions and over a long period of time. *The process for the therapist to track is the idiosyncratic way that each person manages to show an inclination toward some kind of engagement and then how the client manages to spoil it or break the link in some way.* Because each person has a unique developmental organizing experience, the manner of approach and avoidance is likely to be difficult to observe and absolutely unique. It will likely first be noted in transferences to people and situations in the outside world and then eventually will be discernible in the therapeutic relationship.

The Countertransference

It is well known that a therapist struggling to stay connected to a client who perennially disconnects or becomes disoriented tends to feel extremely frustrated and often disoriented himself.[21] It is not just that the client's changing the subject, or turning away, or canceling sessions, or whatever, is in and of itself so frustrating, but that these collapses and ruptures invariably occur at a time when the therapist is experiencing the hopeful possibility of something good happening between them. We can understand this as a transferential fear of connecting on the part of the client and a loss of a sense of continuity for both client and therapist. Sitting with a person living an organizing experience frequently produces a withdrawal and disorientation

---

[21] Hedges, 1992, 1996; Searles, 1965, 1979; Giovacchini 1972, 1975, 1979.

in the therapist as she is not having her own relational needs responded to.

The Resistance

"Resistance" in analytic parlance always means *resistance to fully and consciously experiencing the transference reaction*—not resistance to the therapist or to the therapy. Since the organizing experience trauma was once known in relation to some person in the early environment, what is anticipated and resisted is connecting to someone again only to be re-traumatized. This means that the person will do anything and everything to avoid, veer off, not notice, block, and/or rupture any developing emotional engagement. This resistive disconnecting process has severe consequences for growth in that human beings are programmed for symbiotic attachments from which they can learn more advanced forms of relatedness and disconnection disrupts those learning processes. When a person pervasively living organizing experience attempts to connect interpersonally the connection is always blocked somehow and learning more complex modes of regulating is blocked. With a better developed person who is only experiencing momentary blocks the rupture is likely to occur at some moment when trusting possibilities are available and therefore frightening so that certain kinds of subsequent relational learning are blocked.

The Listening Mode

Our sole analytic goal in working with organizing experiences is finally to intercept possible connections and to find some way to encourage and sustain moments of interpersonal engagement. But since the person living an organizing experience is hell-bent on not allowing an emotional connection to take place our job early in therapy is to find gentle ways of promoting safety and connections. Since people living pervasive organizing experiences often have elaborate reasons and extravagant stories to tell us it is important not to get caught up in the content but to stay focused on the moment-to-moment movement toward and away from interpersonal connections.

The Therapeutic Intervention

From the outset in treatment it is important for us to be on the lookout for all of the ways that the person avoids, veers off, shuts down, changes the subject, and/or ruptures any forming connections. Every intervention needs to be aimed at pulling the client into the interpersonal life of the room and into emotional relatedness with the therapist using whatever means can be mustered. The most important comments will be geared toward showing the client the disconnecting process and attempting to relate it to a lifelong tendency to avoid interpersonal connections and some ways of considering why. This therapeutic task is extremely difficult, painstaking, and requires a great deal of time.[22]

---

[22] In two remarkable books, Jungian analyst Donald Kalsched (1994, 2012) shares similar views and ways of working with primitive experiences that are formulated quite differently in terms of Jungian archetypes.

II. THERAPY WITH
THE SYMBIOTIC-SEPARATING EXPERIENCE

The Developmental Thrust

Babies from four to 24 months are learning emotional relatedness scenarios as they develop personal and stylized attachments with their primary caregivers through processes of mutual affect attunement. [23] Not only are they developing relatedness templates from the standpoint of the baby, but in order to understand the unique personality of the mother/other they must also develop internal relatedness templates that reflect the mother's emotional interactive role in the relationship—that is, infants must learn to identify with the reciprocal parental role. But babies are not only pre-programmed to attach emotionally to their caregivers, they are also pre-programmed to separate and individuate.[24] After the baby has established a reliable attachment pattern, she must also be able to push away as if to say, "I know how you want me to be, but I want to do things my own way, to become my own separate person." Mothers of toddlers are fond of calling this developmental phase "the terrible twos" because there is so much opposition and often anger and aggression expressed on both sides.

---

[23] Margaret Mahler et al. (1968, 1975) have introduced the biological *metaphor* of symbiosis to capture the subjective sense of merger or at-oneness of this period. Alan Schore (1999, 2013, 2015) has captured the neuropsychological essence of this process in his right-brain-to-right-brain mutual affect regulation.

[24] See Slavin & Kleigman, 1997.

The Transference

Every toddler has the task of learning the unique emotional interactions mutually engaged in with their primary caregivers. Thus, in psychotherapy both client and therapist bring their symbiotic and individuating emotional scenarios to color or determine the relationship. Therapists work to set aside their own preferred ways of emotionally interacting in favor of allowing and thereby understanding the well-established scenarios that the client insists on transferring into relationships. Primary attachment patterns involving mutual affect regulation are preverbal so that they cannot possibly be spoken to the therapist but rather they must be enacted by both participants in the therapeutic relationship so that the therapist eventually becomes able to initiate a process of translating the enactments into words—a process often also engaged in by clients. That is, enactments necessarily precede new perceptions of the engagements.[25]

The Countertransference

Since the symbiotic and individuating patterns to be observed and understood in the therapy are preverbal emotional interaction modes, the verbal dialogue between client and therapist will not at first reveal them. Rather, the countertransference will be a crucial informer as the therapist begins to sense the relatedness expectations and demands of the client. It is easy enough to see that some emotional interaction expectations are transferred directly from the client's early experience of their parents. But the role-reversal transferences are less easy to discern. This is where the countertransference may be a very useful tool. That is, the client

---

[25] See D. B. Stern, 1997, 2010, 2015; Bromberg, 2001, 2006, 2011.

begins treating the therapist as he/she was once treated and the therapist begins getting the emotional message that can then be verbalized to the client. These patterns may become discerned and discussed after being enacted in the relationship by the client, the therapist, or by both.[26]

The Resistance

The symbiotic scenarios once learned in primary emotional relationships become deeply embedded in personality and character structure. As such, they are the ways we all seek familiar relationships and are extremely resistant to change. In psychotherapy, once characteristic scenarios have been identified in the transference-countertransference matrix, it will likely be the therapist who confronts the scenarios basically insisting that the person must relinquish them if greater relational freedom is truly desired. Giving up one's familiar life-long ways of engaging people is always a difficult task and necessarily entails some grieving.[27]

The Listening Mode

Symbiotic-separating scenarios are preverbal and cannot become known and narrated until they have first been enacted by two in an intimate interpersonal relationship.[28] In the early phases of replicating and elucidating a particular scenario the therapist seeks to be as empathic and pliable as possible. Using the ongoing question, "What's going on here, anyway?" two can began to discern the way this scenario operates in the here-and-now and the ways

---

[26] Hedges, 1992, 1996, 2013b.
[27] Hedges, 1983/2003.
[28] Bollas 1987, Hedges 2013b.

they are both engaged in perpetuating it.[29] Then begins the analysis of the resistance—the reluctance on one or both parts to relinquish long held emotional interaction patterns.

The Therapeutic Intervention[30]

Therapy begins with the client enacting a variety of nonverbal emotional scenarios that originated in the second year of life. The therapist works to step back and allow the replication of familiar scenarios in the therapeutic relationship *so that they can become known and worked through by the couple.* It is to be expected that in the process the therapist will also be experiencing and enacting emotional templates from his or her early life. An ongoing open dialogue is encouraged based on the question, "What's going on here, anyway?" The therapist often has to point out, "you have found that I can interact with you comfortably in the ways that are most familiar to you—but after all, I am "hired help." If you want to be free of these long-standing patterns you have to dare to develop new ways of relating to me, of experiencing who I am and ultimately of learning to discover the unique qualities of other people.

III. THERAPY WITH THE SELFOTHER EXPERIENCE

The Developmental Thrust

Three-year-olds are preoccupied with confirming their sense of who they are, developing basic talents and skills, and establishing self-esteem. They are forever looking to others to recognize, affirm,

---

[29] Mitchell, 1988, 1993, 1997, 2002.

[30] Otto Kernberg (1975, 1976, 1980) is to be credited for first clarifying the dimensions of "Borderline Personality Organization" that this Symbiotic Experience is derived from. Mahler (1968, 1975) is credited for her development of the early "Symbiosium."

confirm, and inspire a strong cohesive sense of self. The term selfother derives from the fact that they are using an other to perform consolidating functions usually assigned to the self. "See me! See me! Recognize me! Affirm me!" cries the three-year-old.

The Transference

When selfother affirmations and recognitions have been inadequate during the developmental phase of self-consolidation and cohesion, the client searches for this affirmation, confirmation, or inspiration from the relationship with the therapist through what have been called "the mirroring transference," "the twinship transference," and "the idealizing transference."[31]

The Countertransference

When a client is expressing some form of selfother transference therapists often become bored, drowsy, or even irritated or disgusted. This is because they are being used as a part of the client's self-confirmation process and ignored for who they might be as separate independent people.

The Resistance

There is often a reluctance for clients to express their selfother needs for affirmation, confirmation and inspiration. This reluctance is based on the fear that they will feel ashamed for their selfishness or self-centeredness or that they will become enraged for lack of narcissistic recognition. Yet we all need basic recognition and narcissistic supplies throughout our lives in order to continue to

---

[31] Kohut, 1971, 1977.

feel strong, healthy, and worthwhile in our relationships and endeavors.[32]

The Listening Mode

Kohut has done more than anyone to clarify this particular developmental stage advises us to resonate with the client's needs for affirmation, confirmation, and idealization so that the person can resume the growth of their cohesive self. He advises us to extend our empathy the best we can to the experiencing of narcissistic needs. However, sooner or later our empathy will falter or fail and a narcissistic injury will result. It is at that time that we can review with our clients what they were needing from us that they failed to get and the exact nature of their disappointment and disillusionment with us. Over time with empathic failures and repair the client internalizes the therapist's selfother functions in order to be able to regulate her ongoing needs for affirmation and recognition for herself.

The Therapeutic Intervention

Kohut advised empathic attunement to the state of the client's self and the particular needs the client has for selfother recognition. When the sense of self seems to be flagging or fragmenting it is important for the therapist to be able to resonate with the failing selfother functions, thereby bolstering the development of self-cohesion.

---

[32] Benjamin (1988, 1995, 1998) has developed our need for recognition.

IV. THERAPY WITH THE INDEPENDENCE EXPERIENCE

The Developmental Thrust

Four- and five-year-olds who have consolidated a strong sense of self are ready to engage in complex interactions with other independent selves. The model of complex independent interaction is the emotional-triangular relationship. In each significant intimate relationship, the child is working out the problem of "who is who to whom under what conditions? The specimen problem to be worked out under different conditions is, "who am I to Mommy with and without Daddy." "And who am I to Daddy with or without Mommy?" "And who am I when Mommy and Daddy are together and I am left out, alone?" At this age children are capable of repressing painful and otherwise forbidden or overstimulating unwanted impulses and feelings.

The Transference

Most of our lives are spent dealing with triangular relationships with other loved and hated people. Early ambivalent emotional attitudes developed in triangular relationships are regularly transferred into contemporary relationships including the therapeutic relationship. Sometimes the third party is a family or community value or an allegiance that interacts in various ways to influence a twosome. As adolescence and group life develop a cascade of triangular complexities evolve which are regularly transferred into the therapy arena. The most painful feelings here are, of course, those of being left out when we want to be considered, valued, and included.

The Countertransference

When clients are transferring to us independent experiences of a triangular nature many thoughts and feelings may be stimulated in us. But Freud warned us that under such circumstances of independent relating these feelings are usually our own and seldom of any real use to understanding what the client is experiencing. If anything, strong countertransference reactions to an independently relating client are likely to be distracting from whatever triangular situations the client is working on herself.

The Resistance

At this level of development repression of painful and unwanted feelings makes triangular relating easier or simpler for the growing child. The resistance in therapy is to the return of these overstimulating painful, shameful, repressed, or otherwise defended thoughts, impulses and feelings.

The Listening Mode

The therapeutic modality for listening to Independent Self relating is the one *par excellence* that Freud and the classical psychoanalysts have taught us. In classical terms we are urged to allow the client to free associate without judgment as repressed thoughts and feelings return to consciousness. The stance is one of neutrality and remaining equidistance from the forces and functions of id, ego, and superego.

The Therapeutic Intervention

The verbal-symbolic interpretation of resistances to repressed unconscious conflicts is the recommended intervention for

Independent Self relating in which triangular complexities are possible.

The following table in two parts summarizes Part Four on Therapeutic Engagement.

Relational Listening I:
Development, Transference, Countertransference

Age	Developmental Thrust	Transference	Countertransference
> 3yrs	Self and Other Relational Experiences	From Independent, Ambivalently Held Others	Overstimulating Experiences as Distracting or Impediment
24 to 36 Months	Self-consolidating, Recognition Experiences	From Resonating or Injuring Self-Others	Facilitating Experiences of Fatigue, Boredom, and Drowsiness
4 to 24 Months	Symbiotic and Separating Scenarios/ Interactive Experience	From Interacting and Enacting Others– Replication	Resistive Experiences to Replicating Demanding, Dependent Scenarios
± 4 Months	Organizing Merger and Rupturing Experiences	From Engaging and Disengaging Others	Dread and Terror of Unintegrated Experiences

Relational Listening II:
Resistance, Listening Mode, Therapeutic Intervention

Age	Resistance	Listening Mode	Therapeutic Intervention
> 3yrs	To the Return of The Repressed	Evenly Hovering Attention Free Association Equidistance	Interpretive Reflection: Verbal-Symbolic Interpretation
24 to 36 Months	To Experiencing Narcissistic Shame and Narcissistic Rage	Resonance with Self-Affirmation, Confirmation, and Inspiration	Empathic Attunement to Self to Self-Other Resonance
4 to 24 Months	To Assuming Responsibility for Differentiating	Replicating and Renouncing Symbiotic and Separating Scenarios	Replication Standing Against the Symbiotic & Separating Scenarios: Reverberation
± 4 Months	To Bonding Connections and Engagements	Engagement: Connection, Interception, Linking	Focus On and Interception of Disengagements

Part Five

CONCLUSIONS

Most therapists coming out of training and for some time afterward have a difficult time shifting into Interpersonal Relational Listening modes for three reasons. First, psychotherapy training remains dominated by the medical model of mental illness so that beginners are taught to look for symptoms and to form objective diagnoses based on supposed mental pathologies. Secondly, insurance companies have biased treatment preferences in terms of short-term, "empirically validated" cost-effective, objective intervention modes. Thirdly, it takes some time in clinical practice before one realizes that lasting personality change occurs only in the context of relationships—intimate personal relationships and especially the therapeutic one. It takes time to develop such relationships and it takes mutual commitment to the relationship work to yield lasting results. So interest in and the development of Relational Listening skills is late in coming to most career psychotherapists.

Using Levenson's three-part algorithm for psychotherapy, practicing therapists first learn how many complexities there are in setting up the frame, the safety of the therapeutic contract. Then the extended inquiry into relationships—past, present, future—begins according to whatever personal style the therapist has developed in her training and practice. But the limiting relational habits and modes of relating, while often worked on in relationships outside therapy, finally are critically discovered to be operating in the therapeutic relationship itself in the ways the client is experiencing the therapist and what the client hopes for and dreads from the therapist.

I hope that this *Handbook* conveys my belief that the relatedness possibilities of each person vary for a lifetime in complexity from the simple affective exchanges learned in infancy, through complex interactions of childhood, and the socialized solidifications in adolescence and young adulthood. Even in optimal growth at every stage of relational learning we run into obstacles that inhibit our relational growth and have remained internalized to thwart our current relationships.

Some people, of course, were subjected to intense relational traumas along the way, especially in the earliest months and years. It is difficult for these people to continue to grow and diversify their relatedness potentials until these obstacles to relatedness learning are dismantled. Various mindfulness techniques can be very helpful in trying to patch things over using our incredible capacities for brain plasticity. But in the long run no amount of mindfulness training or plasticity will dismantle long-standing relatedness habits and inhibitions. Rather they have to be enacted, lived with and through in an intimate relationship where they can be seen, and allowed to relax their grip on our lives.

As earlier stated, this book is a telegraphic summary of a 45-year project involving hundreds of Southern California therapists of many different therapeutic persuasions. But throughout I have indicated where the ideas are expanded and where rich case illustrations contributed by many therapists can be found. I hope you have enjoyed your read and that you can allow these ideas to take hold in your relatedness possibilities.

Larry Hedges
April, 2018

Appendix

Epistemology and the Creation of Relational Listening Perspectives[33]

From Modern to Post-Modern Possibilities

Something in us wants certainty, demands the best possible fix on reality, experiences discomfort unless we know for sure, insists on finally knowing "the truth" of what's really out there—the so-called "modern" perspective. Psychoanalytic theorizing, like the theorizing that preceded it in the natural and social sciences, has followed this unyielding human demand for certainty into the pursuit of "the true nature of mind"—even though at this point in time it is widely understood that objective certainty, as it has been sought in science is, in principle, an impossibility—the "post-modern perspective." The result is that the psychoanalytic enterprise, after a century of clinical experience and theoretical elaboration, is an ever-expanding, tangled labyrinth of competing and contradictory truths and myths emanating from any number of schools of thought—each religiously purporting in its own way to have a corner on the truth of mental functioning. Lost in the burgeoning body of psychotherapeutic and psychoanalytic work, however, has been the essential epistemology and philosophy of science informing 20th-century thought that reveals the traditional approach to knowledge expansion to be anachronistic and untenable.

---

[33] Adapted from Hedges, 2015.

Back in 1983, with *Listening Perspectives in Psychotherapy* I set out to reformulate a century of psychoanalytic psychology along lines that are more compatible with a contemporary "postmodern" epistemology and philosophy of science—with the hope of liberating psychotherapeutic theory and practice from an obsolete 19th-century "modern" scientific paradigm.

My ongoing studies have reorganized the central concepts of psychotherapeutic practice—transference, resistance, and countertransference—along the lines of *listening to progressively more complex internalized self-and-other relationship possibilities.* This epistemological move makes it possible to conceptualize an infinite set of individualized patternings of relational possibility that can be re-constellated in an endless variety of ways in the context of every psychoanalytic relationship. With the potential data pool thus expanded to an infinity of relational possibilities comparable to the expanded data pool of the other 20th- and 21st-century postmodern sciences, questions can then be entertained as to what perspectives on the forever elusive data of mind one might choose to define at any moment in time, and for what purposes.

Listening Perspectives as Frames for Understanding Relational Experience

The Relational Listening Perspectives approach as I have defined it and others have adapted and expanded it, aids in framing for therapeutic understanding different qualities of internalized interpersonal relatedness experience as they arise in the here-and-now cognitive-emotional-motivational matrix of the therapeutic relationship. Based on the work of the philosophers Wittgenstein (1953), Ryle (1949) , Rorty (1989), and Searle (1992, 2004), I have expanded and elaborated this philosophical and epistemological orientation further in light of quantum and chaos theories.[34] This approach to truths and realities seeks to mitigate against ever assuming or proceeding as if we know or understand with certainty anything that's "really there." This approach to knowledge represents a radical shift in the conception and perception of the interpersonal relatedness experience itself that is seldom fully appreciated.

The Relational Listening Perspectives approach abandons entirely the naïve view that we can ever objectively consider how "things really are" or that the human mind can ever be studied as an isolated unit separate from the biophysical, sociocultural, psycholinguistic, and intersubjective fields in which human beings necessarily live. The perspectival view of truth and reality maintains that all we can ever do with any degree of certainty is to generate systematically helpful points of view, perceptual angles, and/or empathic stances or lenses from which to listen in order to frame (to experience in the broadest possible sense) what people have to tell us and to the ways in which two people engage each other in the here-and-now therapeutic relationship. This way of approaching the psychotherapeutic situation encourages us as professional listeners to experience ourselves as living human participants involved in a full emotional relationship with someone endeavoring to experience, and to express in one way or another, his or her relational life experiences.

The Relational Listening Perspectives approach further encourages us *to formulate* our work in terms of theories that enhance listening and speaking possibilities within a living,

---

[34] Hedges 1992.

breathing, here-and-now relationship, rather than theories that seek to reify or personify concepts or to capture the eternal verities of existence or the true nature of the human mind as objectively defined and viewed in isolation. This approach finds fault with all reified and personified processes—including multiple selves, dissociation, models, and enactments.

The four self-and-other Relational Listening Perspectives considered here have evolved out of more than 100 years of psychoanalytic research that bridge across many existing theories of the mind.

The Four Relational Listening Perspectives

The number and ways of defining Relational Listening Perspectives from which to study the transactions of relational encounters is entirely open-ended and arbitrary. But a century of psychoanalytic study suggests four distinctly different essential Relational Listening Perspectives that have served the purpose of framing self-and-other intersubjective relatedness patterns that operate in the interpersonal field. Traditional "modern" scientific-objective approaches pre-specify in various ways *the presumed nature* of psyche, what kinds *of structures, contents, and events* an analytic observer is likely to see, and the ways in which the analytic search for *transference and resistance memories* are "best" framed.

A more intersubjective Relational Listening Perspective approach simply defines an array of human relatedness possibilities that could serve to frame, for mutual understanding, *whatever* idiosyncratic narratives and narrational interactions become co-constructed so that they emerge for mutual observation in the course of the relationship development.

100

Internalized relatedness patterns from the lived past of each participant, as well as novel configurations emerging from the unique intersubjective engagement of therapy will be an expectable focus of discussion as the therapeutic relationship unfolds. [35] Emotional honesty and limited disclosure of affective experience on the part of the analyst will be an expectable part of the emerging therapeutic relationship.[36] The development of a personal creative style of relating that integrates, like postmodern art, a variety of ideas and interventions into the specific therapeutic exchange will be another expectable aspect of the emergent dialogue.[57] A multiplicity of ways of viewing and working together with the internalized patterns of both people, and the emerging configurations of interactions characteristic of the couple, can also be expected.[37]

The four Relational Listening Perspectives are based on developmental *metaphors* of how a growing child potentially engages and is engaged by emotionally significant others in interpersonal interactions that build internal habits, structures, or patterns of relational expectation. Understanding the general sequence of human relational development allows an understanding of the basis for how subsequent relational patterns necessarily modify earlier habit patterns. Differential framing of each metaphoric level of self and other experience secures for therapeutic study the *patterns, configurations,* and/or *modes* or *habits* of internalized interpersonal interaction that have characterized the past interactions of both participants and that are

[35] Hedges, 1983/2003, 1992, 1996, 2000b, 2013c, 2013d.
[36] Maroda, 1994, 1999; Johnson, 1985, 1987, 1991, 1994.
[37] Stark. 1994, 1997, 2017.

transferred into and resisted conscious awareness and expression in the current mutually developing psychotherapeutic relationship.

Relational Listening Perspectives thus formed do *not* represent a developmental schema, but rather serve to identify a general array of relatedness possibilities lived out each day by all people. Careful study of the Developmental Listening Charts Following Part Four of this *Handbook* reveals a general coherency of approach.

The central idea here is that if we want to empathically engage with a child or a person re-experiencing some pattern of reactions or traumatic adaptations learned in childhood, we have to understand the relatedness level currently in play and respond in kind. For example, an infant may grasp the emotional intent of a speaking adult but the content is essentially incomprehensible. On the other hand, if we speak to an older child or adult as if they were much younger, they are likely to feel infantilized, angered, or insulted. It follows that if a therapeutic strategy depends on shifting cognitions, setting goals, and/or attaining insight when the relatedness patterns, the internalized traumatic adaptations, are currently operating at a much less complex emotional level, then the results of the therapy process will simply be an intellectualized false-self compliance cure rather than relationally transformative.

Physicists tell us that we are actively living in ten or more dimensions while we can only consciously perceive four of them.[38] This means that even the most sophisticated formulations only touch the surface of our deeper beings, of the patterns that operate in the unformulated and unformulatable parts of our personalities and neurological systems, and of the possibilities for

---

[38] Greene, 1999, 2004.

transformation that exist for us. The British psychoanalyst Wilfred Bion came to believe that all transformations—whether developmentally formative or therapeutically re-formative—in "O"—the dimensions of our existence that are unknown and unknowable![39]

The bottom line: we do not know all of the forces that promote our growth or that can be mobilized in overcoming directing internalized experiences—but we assume those forces are within us and working for all of us. What we can do, however, is create perspectives from which to listen to our clients and ourselves in the broadest sense of the word so that whatever internal processes are available to a person will be mobilized in expanding transformations that free that person from the bondage of her or his own internalized developmental traumatic adaptations.

---

[39] Bion, 1962, 1963, 1977.

References

Aron, L. (2001). *A Meeting of Minds.* New York: Routledge.

Benjamin, J. (1988). *The Bonds of Love.* New York: Pantheon Books.

____. (1995). *Like Subjects, Love Objects: Essays on Recognition and Sexual Difference.* New Haven: Yale.

____. (1998). *Shadow of the Other.* New York: Routledge.

Bion, W. R. (1962). *Learning from Experience.* New York: Basic Books.

____. (1963). *Elements of Psycho-Analysis.* New York: Basic Books.

____. (1977). *Second Thoughts.* New York: Jason Aronson.

Boston Change Process Group. (2007). The Foundational Level of Psychodynamic Meaning: Implicit Process in Relation to Conflict, Defense and the Dynamic Unconscious. *Int. J. Psycho-Anal.,* 88:843-860.

Bollas, C. (1987). *The Shadow of the Object: Psychoanalysis of the Unthought Known.* New York: Columbia University Press.

Bromberg, P. (2001). *Standing in the Spaces: Essays on Clinical Process, Trauma and Dissociation.* New York: Routledge.

____. (2006). *Awakening the Dreamer: Clinical Journeys.* New York: Routledge.

____. (2011). *The Shadow of the Tsunami and the Growth of the Relational Mind.* New York: Routledge.

Cozolino, L. (2002). *The Neuroscience of Human Relationships: Attachment and the Developing Social Brain.* New York: W.W. Norton.

____. (2006). *The Neuroscience of Human Relationships: Attachment and the Developing Social Brain.* New York: W.W. Norton

____. (2012).*The Social Neuroscience of Education*: Optimizing Attachment and Learning in the Classroom. New York: Norton.

Damasio, A. (1994). *Descartes' Error.* New York: Grosset/Putnam.

____. (1999). *The Feeling of What Happens.* New York: Harcourt Brace.

____. (2003). *Looking for Spinoza: Joy, Sorrow, and the Feeling Brain.* New York: Harcourt.

Freud, S. (1895). Project for a Scientific Psychology. *Standard Edition* 1:283-390.

_____. (1924). The Dissolution of the Oedipus Complex. *Standard Edition* 19:172-179.

Green, B. (1999). *The Elegant Universe: Superstrings, Hidden Dimensions, and the Quest for the Ultimate Theory.* New York: W.W. Norton.

_____. (2004). *Fabric of the Cosmos: Space, Time, and the Texture of Reality.* New York: Knopf.

Giovacchini, P. L. (1972). *Tactics and Techniques in Psychoanalytic Therapy.* New York: Jason Aronson.

_____. (1975). *Psychoanalysis of Character Disorders.* New York: Jason Aronson.

_____. (1979). *Treatment of Primitive Mental States.* New York: Jason Aronson.

Hedges, L. E. (1983). *Listening Perspectives in Psychotherapy.* Northvale, NJ: Jason Aronson Publishers [Twentieth Anniversary Edition, 2003].

_____. (1992). *Interpreting the Countertransference.* Northvale, NJ: Jason Aronson Publishers.

_____. (1994a). *In Search of the Lost Mother of Infancy.* Northvale, NJ: Jason Aronson Publishers.

_____. (1994b). *Remembering, Repeating, and Working Through Childhood Trauma: The Psychodynamics of Recovered Memories, Multiple Personality, Ritual Abuse, Incest, Molest, and Abduction.* Northvale, NJ: Jason Aronson Publishers.

_____. (1994c). *Working the Organizing Experience: Transforming Psychotic, Schizoid, and Autistic States.* Northvale, NJ: Jason Aronson Publishers.

_____. (1996). *Strategic Emotional Involvement: Using Countertransference Experience in Psychotherapy.* Northvale, NJ: Jason Aronson Publishers.

_____. (2000a). *Facing the Challenge of Liability in Psychotherapy: Practicing Defensively.* Northvale, NJ: Jason Aronson.

_____. (2000b). *Terrifying Transferences: Aftershocks of Childhood Trauma.* Northvale, NJ: Jason Aronson Publishers.

____. (2005). Listening Perspectives for Emotional Relatedness Memories. *Psychoanalytic Inquiry, 25:4, 455-483.*

____. (2010*). Sex in Psychotherapy: Sexuality, Passion, Love, and Desire in the Therapeutic Encounter.* New York: Routledge.

__ (2012a). *Cross-Cultural Encounters.* International Psychotherapy Institute e-Book, freepsychotheapybooks.org

____. (2012b). *Overcoming Relationship Fears.* International Psychotherapy Institute e-Book, freepsychotherapybooks.org.

____. (2013a). *Making Love Last.* International Psychotherapy Institute e-Book, freepsychotherapybooks.org.

____. (2013b). *Overcoming Relationship Fears Workbook.* International Psychotherapy Institute e-Book, freepsychotherapybooks.org.

____. (2013c). *Relational Interventions: Treating Borderline, Bipolar, Schizophrenic, Psychotic, and Characterological Personality Organization.* International Psychotherapy Institute e-Book, freepsychotherapybooks.org.

____. (2013d). *The Relationship in Psychotherapy and Supervision.* International Psychotherapy Institute e-Book, freepsychotherapybooks.org.

____. (2015). *Facing Our Developmental Traumas.* International Psychotherapy Institute e-Book, freepsychotherapybooks.org.

____. (1997). Hedges, L., Hilton, R., Hilton, V., Caudill, B. *Therapists At Risk: Perils of the Intimacy of the Therapeutic Relationship.* Northvale, NJ: Jason Aronson Publishers.

Johnson, S. M. (1985). *Characterological Transformation: The Hard Work Miracle.* New York: Norton.

____. (1987) *Humanizing the Narcissistic Style.* New York: Norton

____. (1991), *The Symbiotic Character.* New York: Norton.

____. (1994). *Character Styles.* New York: Norton.

Kalsched, D. (1994). *The Inner World of Trauma: Archetypal Defenses of the Spirit.* New York: Routledge.

____. (2012). *Trauma and the Soul: A Psycho-Spiritual Approach to Human Development and its Interruption.* New York: Routledge.

Kernberg O. F.(1975). *Borderline Personality Organization*. New York: Jason Aronson.

____. (1976). *Object-Relations Theory and Clinical Psychoanalysis*. New York Jason Aronson.

____. (1980). *Internal World and External Reality*. New York: Jason Aronson.

Kohut, H. (1971). *The Analysis of the Self*. New York: International Universities Press.

____. (1977). *The Restoration of the Self*. New York: International Universities Press.

LeDoux, J. (1996). *The Emotional Brain*. New York: Simon & Schuster.

____. (2002). *The Synaptic Self*. New York: Viking.

Levenson, E. A. (1972, 2005). *The Fallacy of Understanding: An Inquiry into the Changing Structure of Psychoanalysis*. Hillsdale, NJ: The Analytic Press.

____. (1983, 2005). *The Ambiguity of Change: An Inquiry into the Nature of Psychoanalytic Reality*. Hillsdale, NJ: The Analytic Press.

____. (2017). *The Purloined Self*. New York: Routledge.

Mahler, M. (1968). *On Human Symbiosis and the Vicissitudes of Individuation*, Vol. 1, *Infantile Psychosis*. New York: International Universities Press.

__Pine, Fred and Bergman, Anni (1975). *The Psychological Birth of the Human Infant: Symbiosis and Individuation*. New York: Basic Books.

Maroda, K. (1994). *The Power of Countertransference*. Northvale NJ: Aronson.

____. (1999). *Seduction, Surrender, and Transformation*. Hillsdale, NJ: Analytic Press.

McGilchrist, I. (2010). *The Master and His Emissary: The Divided Brain and The Making of The Western World*. New Haven: Yale University Press.

Mitchell, S. (1988). *Relational Concepts in Psychoanalysis*. Cambridge, MA: Harvard University Press.

____. (1993). *Hope and Dread in Psychoanalysis*. New York: Basic Books.

____. (1997). *Influence and Autonomy in Psychoanalysis*. Hillsdale, NJ: The Analytic Press.

____. (2002). *Can Love Last?* NY: W.W. Norton & Co.

Porges, S. (2011). *The Polyvagal Theory: Neurophysiological Foundations of Emotions, Attachment, Communication and Self-Regulation.* New York: Norton.

Rorty, R. (1979). *Philosophy and the Mirror of Nature.* Princeton, NJ: Princeton University Press.

____. (1989). *Contingency, Irony, and Solidarity.* Cambridge, MA: Cambridge University Press.

Ryle, G. (1949). *The Concept of Mind.* New York: Barnes and Noble.

Schore, A. N. (1999). *Affect Regulation and the Origin of the Self: The Neurobiology of Emotional Development.* NY: Lawrence Erlbaum Associates

____. (2003). *Affect Regulation and Disorders of the Self.* New York: W. W. Norton & Company.

____. (2012). *The Art and Science of Psychotherapy.* New York: Norton.

Searle, J. R. (1992). *The Rediscovery of the Mind.* Cambridge, MA: The MIT Press.

____. (2004). *Mind: A Brief Introduction.* New York: Oxford University Press.

Searles, H. (1965). *Collected Papers on Schizophrenia and Related Subjects.* New York: International Universities Press.

____. (1979). *Countertransference and Related Subjects. Selected Papers.* New York: International Universities Press.

Siegel, D. J. (1999). *The Developing Mind: How Relationships and the Brain Interact to Shape Who We Are.* New York: The Guilford Press.

____. (2007). *The Mindful Brain.* New York: W.W. Norton.

____. (2010). *Mindsight: The New Science of Personal Transformation.* New York: Random House.

____. (2012). *Pocket Guide to Interpersonal Neurobiology.* New York: Norton.

Slavin, M. O., and Kriegman, O. (1992). *The Adaptive Design of the Human Psyche.* New York: Guilford.

Stark, M. (1994). *Working with Resistance.* New York: Aronson.

_____. (1997). *Modes of Therapeutic Action*. New York: Aronson.

_____. (2017). *Relentless Hope: The Refusal to Grieve*. The International Psychotherapy Institute, freepsychotherapybooks.org.

Stern, D. B. (1997). *Unformulated Experience: From Dissociation to Imagination in Psychoanalysis*. Hillsdale, NJ: The Analytic Press.

_____. (2010). *Partners in Thought: Working with Unformulated Experience, Dissociation, and Enactment*. New York: Routledge.

_____. (2015). *Relational Freedom: Working in the Interpersonal Field*. New York: Routledge.

Stern, D. N. (1985). *The Interpersonal World of the Infant*. New York: Basic Books.

_____. (2004). *The Present Moment in Psychotherapy and Everyday Life*. New York: W.W. Norton and Company.

Winnicott, D. W. (1949). Birth Memories, Birth Trauma, and Anxiety. In *Through Paediatrics to Psychoanalysis* (1975). London: Hogarth Press.

_____. (1969) The Use of an Object. *International Journal of Psycho-analysis. 50:711-716.*

___ (1971). *Playing and Reality*. New York: Basic Books.

Wittgenstein, L. (1953). *Philosophical Investigations*. (G.E.M. Anscombe, tr.) New York: Macmillan Publishing Co., Inc.

Young-Bruehl, E., and Dunbar, C. (2009). *One Hundred Years of Psychoanalysis: A Timeline: 1900-2000*. Toronto, Canada: Caversham Productions.

About the Author

Lawrence Hedges, Ph.D., Psy.D., ABPP, began seeing patients in 1966 and completed his training in child psychoanalysis in 1973. Since that time his primary occupation has been training and supervising psychotherapists, individually and in groups, on their most difficult cases at the Listening Perspectives Study Center in Orange, California. Dr. Hedges was the Founding Director of the Newport Psychoanalytic Institute in 1983 where he continues to serve as supervising and training analyst. Throughout his career, Dr. Hedges has provided continuing education courses for psychotherapists throughout the United States and abroad. He has consulted or served as expert witness on more than 400 complaints against psychotherapists in 20 states and has published 21 books on various topics of interest to psychoanalysts and psychoanalytic psychotherapists, three of which have received the Gradiva Award for the best psychoanalytic book of the year. During the 2009 centennial celebration of the International Psychoanalytic Association, his 1992 book, *Interpreting the Countertransference*, was named one of the key contributions in the relational track during the first century of psychoanalytics. In 2015 Dr. Hedges was distinguished by being awarded honorary membership in the American Psychoanalytic Association for his many contributions to psychoanalysis.

Photograph courtesy Marcie Bell

Other Books Authored and Edited by Lawrence Hedges

Listening Perspectives in Psychotherapy (1983;
Revised Edition 2003; 40th Anniversary Edition 2022)

In a fresh and innovative format Hedges organizes an exhaustive overview of contemporary psychoanalytic and object relations theory and clinical practice. "In studying the Listening Perspectives of therapists, the author has identified himself with the idea that one must sometimes change the Listening Perspective and also the interpreting, responding perspective." –Rudolf Ekstein, Ph.D. Contributing therapists: Mary Cook, Susan Courtney, Charles Coverdale, Arlene Dorius, David Garland, Charles Margach, Jenna Riley, and Mary E. Walker. Now available in a 40th Anniversary edition, the book has become a classic in the field.

Interpreting the Countertransference (1992)

Dr. Hedges boldly studies countertransference as a critical tool for therapeutic understanding. "Hedges clearly and beautifully delineates the components and forms of countertransference and explicates the technique of carefully proffered countertransference informed interventions ... [He takes the view] that all countertransferences, no matter how much they belong to the analyst, are unconsciously evoked by the patient." –James Grotstein, M.D. Contributing therapists: Anthony Brailow, Karen K. Redding, and Howard Rogers. During the 2009 centennial celebrations of The International Psychoanalytic Association *Interpreting the Countertransference* was named one of the key contributions in the relational track during the first century of psychoanalytics.

In Search of the Lost Mother of Infancy (1994)

"Organizing transferences" in psychotherapy constitute a living memory of a person's earliest relatedness experiences and failures. Infant research and psychotherapeutic studies from the past two decades now make it possible to define for therapeutic analysis the manifestations of early contact traumas. A history and summary of the Listening Perspective approach to psychotherapy introduces the book. Contributing therapists: Bill Cone, Cecile Dillon, Francie Marais, Sandra Russell, Sabrina Salayz, Jacki Singer, Sean Stewart, Ruth Wimsatt, and Marina Young.

Working the Organizing Experience:
Transforming Psychotic, Schizoid, and Autistic States (1994)

Hedges defines in a clear and impelling manner the most fundamental and treacherous transference phenomena, the emotional experiences retained from the first few months of life. Hedges describes the infant's attempts to reach out and form organizing connections to the interpersonal environment and how those attempts may have been ignored, thwarted, and/or rejected. He demonstrates how people live out these primitive transferences in everyday significant relationships and in the psychotherapy relationship. A critical history of psychotherapy with primitive transferences is contributed by James Grotstein and a case study is contributed by Frances Tustin.

Remembering, Repeating, and Working Through Childhood Trauma:
The Psychodynamics of Recovered Memories, Multiple Personality, Ritual Abuse, Incest, Molest, and Abduction (1994)

Infantile focal as well as strain trauma leave deep psychological scars that show up as symptoms and memories later in life. In psychotherapy people seek to process early experiences that lack ordinary pictoral and narrational representations through a variety of forms of transference and dissociative remembering such as multiple personality, dual relating, archetypal adventures, and false accusations against therapists or other emotionally significant people. "Lawrence Hedges makes a powerful and compelling argument for why traumatic memories recovered during psychotherapy need to be taken seriously. He shows us how and why these memories must be dealt with in thoughtful and responsible ways and not simply uncritically believed and used as tools for destruction." – Elizabeth F. Loftus, Ph.D. Nominated for Gradiva Best Book of the Year Award.

Strategic Emotional Involvement:
Using the Countertransference in Psychotherapy (1996)

Following an overview of contemporary approaches to studying countertransference responsiveness, therapists tell moving stories of how their work came to involve them deeply, emotionally, and not always safely with clients. These comprehensive, intense, and honest reports are the first of their kind ever to be collected and published. Contributing therapists: Anthony Brailow, Suzanne Buchanan, Charles Coverdale, Carolyn Crawford, Jolyn Davidson, Jacqueline Gillespie, Ronald Hirz, Virginia Hunter, Gayle Trenberth, and Sally Turner-Miller.

Therapists at Risk:
Perils of the Intimacy of the Therapeutic Relationship (1997)

Lawrence E. Hedges, Robert Hilton, and Virginia Wink Hilton, long-time trainers of psychotherapists, join hands with attorney O. Brandt Caudill in this *tour de force* which explores the multitude of personal, ethical, and legal risks involved in achieving rewarding transformative connections in psychotherapy today. Relational intimacy is explored through such issues as touching, dualities in relationship, interfacing boundaries, sexuality, countertransference, recovered memories, primitive transferences, false accusations against therapists, and the critical importance of peer support and consultation. The authors clarify the many dynamic issues involved, suggest useful ways of managing the inherent dangers, and work to restore our confidence in and natural enjoyment of the psychotherapeutic process.

Terrifying Transferences:
Aftershocks of Childhood Trauma (2000)

There is a level of stark terror known to one degree or another by all human beings. It silently haunts our lives and occasionally surfaces in therapy. It is this deep-seated fear—often manifest in dreams or fantasies of dismemberment, mutilation, torture, abuse, insanity, rape, or death—that grips us with the terror of being lost forever in time and space or controlled by hostile forces stronger than ourselves. Whether the terror is felt by the client or by the therapist, it has a disorienting, fragmenting, crippling power. How we can look directly into the face of such terror, hold steady, and safely work it through is the subject of *Terrifying Transferences*. Contributing therapists: Linda Barnhurst, John Carter, Shirley Cox, Jolyn Davidson, Virginia Hunter, Michael Reyes, Audrey Seaton-Bacon, Sean Stewart, Gayle Trenberth, and Cynthia Wygal. Gradiva Award Best Book of the Year.

Facing the Challenge of Liability in Psychotherapy:
Practicing Defensively (2000, Revised 2017)

In this litigious age, all psychotherapists must protect themselves against the possibility of legal action; malpractice insurance is insufficient and does not begin to address the complexity and the enormity of this critical problem. In this book, Lawrence E. Hedges urges clinicians to practice defensively and provides a course of action that equips them to do so. After working with over a hundred psycho-therapists and attorneys who have fought unwarranted legal and ethical complaints from clients, he has made the fruits of his work available to all therapists. In addition to identifying those patients prone to presenting legal problems, Dr.

Hedges provides a series of consent forms (on the accompanying disk), a compelling rationale for using them, and a means of easily introducing them into clinical practice. This book is a wake-up call, a practical, clinically sound response to a frightening reality, and an absolute necessity for all therapists in practice today. Now available in a revised and updated edition. Gradiva Award Best Book of the Year.

Sex in Psychotherapy: Sexuality, Passion, Love, and Desire in the Therapeutic Encounter (2010)

This book takes a psychodynamic approach to understanding recent technological and theoretical shifts in the field of psychotherapy. Hedges provides an expert overview and analysis of a wide variety of new perspectives on sex, sexuality, gender, and identity; new theories about sex's role in therapy; and new discoveries about the human brain and how it works. Therapists will value Hedges's unique insights into the role of sexuality in therapy, which are grounded in the author's studies of neurology, the history of sexuality, transference, resistance, and countertransference. Clinicians will also appreciate his provocative analyses of influential perspectives on sex, gender, and identity, and his lucid, concrete advice on the practice of therapeutic listening. This is an explosive work of tremendous imagination and scholarship. Hedges speaks the uncomfortable truth that psychotherapy today often reinforces the very paradigms that keep patients stuck in self-defeating, frustrating behavior. He sees sexuality as a vehicle for both therapists and patients to challenge what they think they know about the nature of self and intimacy. This book is a must-read for anyone interested in understanding 21st-century human beings—or in better understanding themselves and their sexuality.

Cross-Cultural Encounters: Bridging Worlds of Difference (2012)

This book is addressed to everyone who regularly encounters people from other cultural, ethnic, socioeconomic, linguistic, and ability groups. Its special focus, however, is aimed at counselors, therapists, and educators since their daily work so often involves highly personal cross-cultural interactive encounters. The running theme throughout the book is the importance of cultivating an attitude of tentative and curious humility and openness in the face of other cultural orientations. I owe a great debt to the many students, clients, and friends with diverse backgrounds who over the years have taught me how embedded I am in my own cultural biases. And who have helped me find ways of momentarily transcending those biases in order to bridge to an inspiring and illuminating intimate personal connection.

Overcoming Our Relationship Fears (2012)

We are all aware that chronic tension saps our energy and contributes to such modern maladies as high blood pressure and tension headaches, but few of us realize that this is caused by muscle constrictions that started as relationship fears in early childhood and live on in our minds and bodies. Overcoming Our Relationship Fears is a user-friendly roadmap for healing our relationships by dealing with our childhood fear reflexes. It is replete with relationship stories to illustrate each fear and how we individually express them. Dr. Hedges shows how to use our own built-in "Aliveness Monitor" to gauge our body's reaction to daily interactions and how they trigger our fears. Exercises in the book will help us release these life-threatening constrictions and reclaim our aliveness with ourselves and others.

Overcoming Our Relationship Fears: WORKBOOK (2013)

Developed to accompany Dr. Hedges's *Overcoming Relationship Fears*, this workbook contains a general introduction to the seven relationship fears that are a part of normal human development along with a series of exercises for individuals and couples who wish to learn to how to release their Body-Mind-Relationship fear reflexes. An Aliveness Journal is provided for charting the way these fears manifest in relationships and body maps to chart their location in each person's body.

The Relationship in Psychotherapy and Supervision (2013)

The sea-change in our understanding of neurobiology, infant research, and interpersonal/relational psychology over the past two decades makes clear that we are first and foremost a relational species. This finding has massive implications for the relational processes involved in teaching and supervising psychotherapy. Clinical theory and technique can be taught didactically. But relationship can only be learned through careful attention to the supervisory encounter itself. This advanced text surveys the psychodynamic and relational processes involved in psychotherapy and supervision.

Making Love Last: Creating and Maintaining Intimacy in Long-term Relationships (2013)

We have long known that physical and emotional intimacy diminish during the course of long-term relationships. This book deals with the questions, "Why romance fades over time?" And "What can we do about it?" Relational psychologists, neuropsychologists, and anthropologists have devoted the last two decades to the study of these questions with never before available research tools. It is now clear that we are genetically predisposed to search out intersubjective intimacy from birth but that cultural systems of child rearing seriously limit our possibilities for rewarding interpersonal relationships. Anthropological and neurological data suggests that over time we have been essentially a serially monogamous species with an extraordinary capacity for carving out new destinies for ourselves. How can we come to grips with our genetic and neurological heritage while simultaneously transcending our relational history in order to create and sustain exciting romance and nurturing love in long-term relationships? Making Love Last surveys research and theory suggesting that indeed we have the capacity and the means of achieving the lasting love we long for in our committed relationships.

Relational Interventions:
Treating Borderline, Bipolar, Schizophrenic, Psychotic, and Characterological Personality Organization (2013)

Many clinicians dread working with individuals diagnosed as borderline, bipolar, schizophrenic, psychotic, and character disordered. Often labeled as "high risk" or "difficult", these relational problems and their interpersonal manifestations often require long and intense transformative therapy. In this book Dr. Hedges explains how to address the nature of personality organization in order to flow with—and eventually to enjoy—working at early developmental levels. Dr. Hedges speaks to the client's engagement/disengagement needs, using a relational process-oriented approach, so the therapist can gauge how much and what kind of therapy can be achieved at any point and time.

Facing Our Cumulative Developmental Traumas (2015)

It has now become clear that Cumulative Developmental Trauma is universal. That is, there is no way to grow up and walk the planet without being repeatedly swallowed up by emotional and relational demands from other people. When we become confused, frightened, and overwhelmed our conscious and unconscious minds seek remedies to deal with the situation. Unfortunately, many of the solutions developed in response to intrusive events turn into habitual fear reflexes that get in our way later in life, giving rise to post traumatic stress and relational inhibitions…. This book is about freeing ourselves from the cumulative effects of our life's many relational traumas and the after-effects of those traumas that continue to constrict our capacities for creative, spontaneous, and passionate living.

The Call of Darkness:
A Relational Listening Approach to Suicide Intervention (2018)

The White House has declared suicide to be a national and international epidemic and has mandated suicide prevention training for educational and health workers nationwide. *The Call of Darkness* was written in response to that mandate and begins with the awareness that our ability to predict suicide is little better than chance and that at present there are no consistently reliable empirically validated treatment techniques to prevent suicide. However, in the past three decades much has been learned about the dynamics of suicide and promising treatment approaches have been advanced that are slowly yielding clinical as well as empirical results.

In this book, Dr. Hedges presents the groundbreaking work on suicidality of Freud, Jung, Menninger and Shneidman as well as the more recent work of Linehan, Kernberg, Joiner and the attachment theorists along with the features in common that these treatment approaches seem to share. He puts forth a Relational Listening approach regarding the origins of suicidality in a relational/ developmental context and will consider their implications for treating, and managing suicidality. The tendencies towards blame and self-blame on the part of survivors raise issues of professional responsibility. Dr Hedges discusses accurate assessment, thorough documentation, appropriate standards of care, and liability management.

Terror in Psychotherapy: The New Zealand Lectures (2020)

Contemporary neuroscience, infant research, and relational psychotherapy make clear that we are a relational species—that our brain and neurological systems actually organize in the first year of life depending on the relationships that are and are not available. By the second year of life a symbiotic interaction, characterized by mutual affect regulation and mutual attachment experiences, is becoming established. In *Terror in Psychotherapy*, Dr. Lawrence Hedges demonstrates how trauma experienced during these "organizing" and "symbiotic" levels of relational development stimulate fear, anxiety, and terror that have consequences for later relationships—in extreme forms laying the foundation for suicide and homicide. A series of case vignettes illustrate how early relational intrusive trauma produce terror in transference and counter-transference experiencing.

The Relational Approach in Psychotherapy:
  The China Lectures (2023)

Although virtually all psychological theories and schools of thought now acknowledge the importance of the relationship in psychotherapy, the relationship itself is conceptualized in various ways. In this book, a ten-lecture series presented in ZhengDou, China as a continuing education program to hundreds of psychotherapists, Dr. Larry Hedges surveys a 50-year clinical research program into the nature of relationship based on the therapeutic experience of and contributions from over 400 practitioners. With a foreword by Dr. Marty Klein.

www.ingramcontent.com/pod-product-compliance
Lightning Source LLC
Chambersburg PA
CBHW031521270326
41930CB00006B/467

* 9 7 8 0 9 9 9 4 5 4 7 2 5 *